SEXUAL *POWER*

REBECCA ROSENBLAT

Relationship & Sexuality Therapist, TV & Radio Host

Library and Archives Canada
Cataloguing in Publication

Rosenblat, Rebecca, author
    **Sexual power : you've got it - now use it / Rebecca
Rosenblat.**

ISBN 978-1-897453-44-5 (pbk.)

    **1. Sex (Psychology). 2. Sex--Social aspects. 3. Sex-
-Political aspects. I. Title.**

BF692.R68 2014   155.3   C2014-906507-8

Cover design/realization Donovan Davie: 519-501-2375
Front Cover photograph courtesy Shutterstock
Back cover photo courtesy of Patrik Jandak - Jandak
Photography - www.photojandak.com

First Edition. 144 pages. All rights reserved.
Published October 15, 2014
Manor House Publishing Inc.
www.manor-house.biz (905) 648-2193

We acknowledge the financial support of the Government of
Canada through the Canada Book Fund (CBF) for this project.
Cover design/realization Donovan Davie: 519-501-2375

Other books by Rebecca Rosenblat: *Smooth as Silk;
An Eastern Seduction; Broken Promises; How to Drive
your Lover Wild with Pleasure; Seducing Your Man*

*Dedicated to Joe, David and Josh,
for always believing in me, so I could
make my dreams come true!*

Acknowledgments

Many thanks to all those who opened up their hearts to me and trusted me enough to help them gain self esteem, become empowered, and change the course of their lives.

Special thanks as well to Paulina for always being an inspiration; Gali for reminding me of the importance of magic; Sonja for teaching me the value of laughing at life when there's nothing else to do; Del for emphasizing the value of learning from our mistakes; and Slavka and Lyndsay for showing me what women need in their vulnerable moments. Without you all, this book would be incomplete.

And of course loads of gratitude to my family for supporting me, my publisher Michael B. Davie for approaching me to write a long overdue book, and Dr. Jane Greer for taking time out of her busy schedule to write the Foreword; as she always says, "You can always get what you want, if you're in the know!" - precisely what I hope my book will do for you!

Foreword

Sexual Power… it sounds so simple to access your sexuality and have it empower you in your identity as a woman, providing you with a source of well-being and joy. However, in reality, the pressure of that can often bring about just the opposite. When people put these two words together they can unleash a whole spectrum of feelings, emotions and energy that if not clearly understood can and do wreak havoc as well as despair on your sexual self-esteem. With this in mind, Rebecca Rosenblatt wrote *Sexual Power* to give you the key to use to turn on your sexual engine so that you can experience pleasure, satisfaction and enjoy your life journey going forward in a totally and completely fulfilling way.

The first step is to really "get" the concept of Sexual Power and what it means to you. By presenting a completely integrated and unified voice from all of the recognized experts in the field of sexuality, *Sexual Power* will help you find your voice and speak your sexual truth. To this objective, the book covers the full sexual range from Naomi Wolf and *The Beauty Myth* to multiple research studies including Doctors Meston and Buss, *Why Women Have Sex*, so you can clearly understand your own personal sexual stakes. In other words, you can come to realize what you stand to gain by exercising your sexual power positively, as well as what you stand to lose by losing touch with this vital life force within us all. This ground-breaking book is your road map to enhancing eroticism rather than being disconnected from desire. By challenging the myths and the messages that have imprisoned, trapped, confined and limited women for too long, it offers the clarity and understanding necessary for each woman to redefine her working definition of her personal sexual identity. With this, it becomes possible to then carry this perspective and wisdom into a personal relationship where sexual dynamics abound. Additionally, Rebecca offers you a front row seat into the complexity of her work with couples by sharing various aspects and interventions that she has used. You get to experience the intricacy of sexual intimacy that plays out between two people, combined with the wisdom and wonder of the change she facilitates. The insight and perspective she gives is an understanding that you can equip yourself with and carry into your relationship to create your own sexual shifts. She leaves no stone unturned, capturing the whole range of feelings sex can trigger ranging from pain, rejection, satisfaction, confidence, pleasure and more.

I've had the privilege and pleasure over the past few years to collaborate with Rebecca, who has joined me as a regular guest on my *Let's Talk Sex* radio show at HealthyLife.net, where we have honest, cutting-edge discussions about sex and intimacy. Our joint segment "Opening Closed Doors" was a chance for a new type of conversation, one that gives listeners the rare opportunity to hear from not just one, but two relationship experts on what really goes on behind closed doors. As soon as I met Rebecca when she was first just a guest on my show, I could tell she was bright and knowledgeable. We had an instant connection, dare I say chemistry? She stood out from the numerous other sexuality experts I had welcomed onto my show with her eloquence and savvy, and I decided to make her a regular contributor so my listeners could continue to benefit from her talent. It is that talent, as well as the chemistry I just mentioned, that you will find in this life-changing book. With *Sexual Power* in your hands, you now will be able to open the door to your sexuality, a door that you might not have even realized was closed before reading this book.

The goal of *Sexual Power* is to give you the personal power to say yes to yourself and feel good about that when it comes to sex and sexuality, rather than feeling bad about yourself. This entails being able to experience pleasure in all aspects of your sexual expression including your appearance from something as small as putting on lipstick to strutting your stuff! The most essential element is that whatever your action may be you are doing it by choice, one that you are making for yourself and thereby can take ownership of. When you do this, you free yourself from guilt, blame and judgment while stripping shame as well so that you will not feel objectified or used in any sexual experience you share.

When you embrace and own your power you evolve into a woman with courage and confidence who can experience, and most important, make sense of all her senses. With that you heighten all sensations so that ultimately you can talk your talk and walk your walk with inner and outer sexiness. Patti Labelle sang about it in her number one song *New Attitude*, and that's exactly what it's about: launching your new attitude so that you can tune into your own desire and sing your own sexual song.

To make this happen, Rebecca encourages every woman to become her own Diva and guides you with the specific steps to take so that you can. Becoming a Diva is to be a woman who takes charge, is in control, makes choices about what she wants as well as what she doesn't want, and most significantly is emotionally free and ready to be sexually playful. The power of *Sexual Power* is that will help you liberate your sexual soul so that you can do just that. Now is the time to start your engine, rev up your sexual sizzle, and become a DIVA: Diving Into Vitality Abounding! It's yours for the taking!
- **Dr. Jane Greer**

Contents

Introduction

Our sexuality can be the container of greatest joy or sorrow, pain or pleasure, depending upon how power*ful* or power*less* it makes us feel. It can present itself in simple ways – like sex appeal giving one an upper hand – or complex interactions, involving titillating sex scandals or painful sexual trauma.

But like it or not, this powerful force that's become the synecdoche for myriad things – used to sell anything from libations to cars – exercises its omnipotent force in most aspects of our lives, on a daily basis.

And it's a lot more convoluted than we realize, because the same stimulus can impact people in different ways. A case in point: the woman with body image issues who can become unglued and turned off by Victoria's Secret commercials, versus the sex addict who may get sexually triggered and aroused by the same, to the point of losing all control.

Sexual power can titillate without touching, using erotic energy that exudes a tsunami of sexual tension greater than the physical build up before a genital orgasm. It's what dances upon the spectrum of power play between "yes" and "no", drenched with possibilities. Small wonder vitality depends upon this force, explaining why people give into it at a risk to all that they *are* and all that they *have*.

From boardrooms to bedrooms, no other force can manipulate our thought processes like sexual power can – many a nation has been led to war, many powerhouses brought to their knees, defenselessly, at the hands of unexceptional women using their sexual power.

It stands to reason then, that understanding the machinations of this force can give one an upper edge, even over fame and fortune, creating an unparalleled level playing field for average individuals – unaccustomed to equality – who can use it to their distinct advantage, tilting the odds in their favour.

Dr. Catherine Hakim, a renowned sociologist and author of *Honey Money: The Power of Erotic Capital* (1), refers to sexual power as erotic capital. According to Dr. Hakim:

> *"Erotic capital combines beauty, sex appeal, liveliness, a talent for dressing well, charm, social skills, and sexual competence. And rather than degrading those who employ it, erotic capital represents a powerful and potentially equalizing tool – one that we scorn only to our detriment."*

Hakim believes that the reason some people seem to lead charmed lives – people want to be around them, doors open for them – is because of the power of erotic capital, the overlooked human asset that is at the heart of how we work, interact, make money, succeed and conduct our relationships.

She feels that it's just as influential in our lives as riches, education, and connection. And seeing that our culture is becoming more and more sexualized, the importance of erotic capital will only continue to grow; which in turn will change the role of women in society – since they have more sexual power than men – revolutionizing the power structures in almost everything we do.

Small wonder men and women learn to exploit sexual power in all areas of life.

*   *   *

Part I of the book will cover different forms of sexual power and how they impact various aspects of our day to day living – both professionally as well as personally.

Part II will address how we can wield that knowledge in healthy ways, to gain an advantage in a world where we're either using it or losing it – possibly to someone else.

We need to give ourselves the permission to embrace the phenomenon that's very much at play in every facet of our lives, so we can work *with* it instead of having it work *against* us.

After all, knowledge is power, as is sex, making sexual knowledge the ultimate tour de force!

Praise for *Sexual **Power***

"Sexual Power cuts through the clutter of interpersonal complexities as to what sexuality is and how we involve it in our lives. It's a brilliant and honest application.

Sexual Power is a true powerhouse of knowledge and perspective in understanding the complexities of sexuality and how to apply it to our lives. It embraces bold honesty and opens your perspective to how sexuality can be used in today's world.

Sexual Power fully engulfs you with raw, honest brilliance. Connective and beyond powerful, it is a strong sensual voice of influence and truth.

Sexual Power combines warm understandings of hot topics by addressing cold truths. Brilliant!"

- **Jaime Silk**, Therapist & Self-Esteem Advocate

PART I
UNDERSTANDING
SEXUAL POWER

Chapter 1

Sexual Power at Play

I remember my first summer working at a psychiatric hospital. I ended up acquiring a medical student who was doing a rotation in psychiatry.

While my analytical brain used scientific algorithms to understand the human mind, his brain employed kaleidoscopic thinking, where each perspective was more colourful than the one prior.

It wasn't long before we ended up spending our lunch hours on a picnic bench, with our bare feet planted where our derrieres should've been, doing what most psych researchers do – observe people.

My logic was limited to what made sense, his observations weren't bound by any such thing. So I tried to open up my mind and wrap my head around his comments; but with each new entry my thinking got twisted around, like a Rubik's Cube contorted in a confusing manner. It was then that I realized that I had to shelve my preconceived, politically correct notions, and just watch and learn.

What fascinated him the most was how various females from different backgrounds and socioeconomic statuses all somehow ended up presenting themselves in similar ways, when they were trying to be alluring – the strut, the hair flip, the makeup – strongly indicating that our sexual presentation is more nature, less nurture, implying an evolutionary advantage.

That said, he was convinced that what nature provides nurture refines, so we may use it to our maximum advantage.

But I had a hard time buying that we could actually fine-tune our raw sexuality and use it to feel empowered, even though he'd spent the entire summer trying to convince me of it.

*   *   *

Fast forward to a winter in the future. It was a brutally cold night when my partner and I decided to venture out to one of New York City's hottest, most-happening places.

The lineup to get in extended a few blocks, with spotlights crisscrossing the sky to invite an even bigger multitude, since the club was hosting *Playgirl*'s Hottest Centerfold contest. I couldn't imagine a two hour wait in my high heels and low neckline, both of which spelled excruciating discomfort, so I wanted to leave.

But just then, a big bouncer came around, pointed at me, and said "You!" in an intimidating voice that matched his stature. I was terrified, since he'd just passed over a hundred people and singled me out for some reason. I pointed to my chest and barely mouthed "Me?" hoping that he'd made a mistake. He responded gruffly, "Yes, you – come with me."

Afraid of asking any questions, I just followed him, my partner in tow.

By now my fear had metastasized to the rest of my body and started to make me feel warm, thanks to a racing heart, flushed cheeks, and my sore feet revived for fight or flight – all good, considering the state that I was in.

And then it happened: he opened up the red and gold rope on the red carpet and let me in – to the VIP area no less.

Everything seemed to be going down in slow motion at that point. I was beyond puzzled, still unable to speak. He looked at my face and said, "Beautiful people never have to wait."

My partner was right behind me.

The bouncer put his beefy paw on his chest, to stop him. All I had to do was whisper "Please ... he's with me" to get him aboard.

The bouncer responded with a disappointed "Oh" and let him in as well, while hordes of people at the front of the lineup protested – not that it had any impact on him.

And that started a trend for my partner, who began asking me to use my "sexual power" whenever he felt the need – getting into A List parties and clubs, nabbing the best tables in restaurants without reservations, getting out of moving violations, and whatnot. I finally got what my medical student was trying to teach me.

The first time it happened I wasn't even aware of it, since I wasn't actively trying to do anything, but it was equally effective – and possibly more so – when I did it consciously and shamelessly at my partner's request, much to my chagrin.

Seeing my sexual power work every single time, I became even more excited to be a woman than I already was. I wanted to champion female sexuality in its numerous forms, and the power it represented.

Right then, right there, I finally got Naomi Wolf's quote from *The Beauty Myth* (2):

"A consequence of female self-love is that the woman grows convinced of her social worth. Her love for her body will be unqualified, which is the basis of female identification. If a woman loves her own body, she doesn't begrudge what other women do with theirs; if she loves femaleness, she champions its rights."

Ironically, even though a premium value is placed on female sex appeal, when a woman invests in it she's seen as vain, shallow, and superficial – by other women no less.

Could it be that those women are unable to love their own femaleness; or could it be that they fear what they yearn, because of the power it represents, making it the ultimate currency?

Chapter 2

The Sex Trade (Off)

Dr. Cindy Meston (a clinical psychologist) and Dr. David Buss (an evolutionary psychologist) interviewed over a 1,000 women around the world for their book *Why Women Have Sex* (3), and managed to come up with 237 distinct reasons, including, money, drugs, bartering, promotion, revenge, capturing or poaching a partner, making themselves feel good, getting rid of a headache, and many other unpredictable reasons, with love being further down the line than expected.

According to the authors, most women enjoy their sexiness for all the benefits it provides, above and beyond the physical and the emotional. They referred to it as "sexual economics" and dedicated an entire chapter to it. Specific examples of the phenomenon include everything from getting a partner to take out the garbage, to securing free dinners or getting expensive gifts.

Another study out of University of Michigan – an "elite institution of higher learning" – reported something along the same lines, i.e. that many women are motivated to have sex to get things they want, not necessarily because they're sexually or romantically attracted to the person they're sleeping with. What that tells us is, the power of sex is the real deal, since it can be used to obtain results. But sexual power doesn't necessarily imply having sex to get what you want.

Sexual Power is more about using the power of your sensuality and sexual expression to titillate the imagination without ever having to cross the "skin barrier". Regardless, many will use sex either directly or indirectly to seal the deal, since they feel it's the fair thing to do.

Examples of the former include, sugar babies exploiting their sexual power to get sugar daddies to fund an expensive lifestyle; or college students working as exotic dancers, call-girls, or prostitutes, to raise tuition in the fastest way possible, so they can "have enough time left over for studying, versus waiting tables for hours on end, making minimum wage."

A case in point: Gabriela da Silva, author of *The Pleasure Is All Ours* (4), written under the pseudonym Lola Benvenutti, used prostitution to pay her way through college. And she wanted to be clear that it was a personal choice, not something she got thrown into due to an abusive and traumatic past. Toward that end, in an interview after her book launch, she drew a distinction between her book and a 2006 novel by former prostitute Rachel Pacheco, later made into the hit Brazilian movie *Bruna Surfistinha*. She said, "The way it was presented was about the prostitute as a victim, who suffers, but sex for me has always been very good. I do everything to have pleasure."

That said, I'd be reticent if I didn't point out that many sex trade workers do come from a place of past trauma, who may well experience what Pacheco suggested; but it's good to know that that isn't always the case. In fact, for some it represents a shift in sexual power. Examples of indirect use of sexual power include, countless negotiations in romantic relationships.

I've seen many highly accomplished men and women on their insecure knees, begging younger/sexier mates for their affection, losing their immense power in various arenas to the sexual power of significantly less accomplished persons, who use it rather effectively.

An amazing woman I know and respect manages to get an invite to any and every exclusive event she wants to attend, so she can network with the most powerful and influential people in the world. Not only that, she manages to get a hot outfit to wear to each event. She'll find someone who has an invite and hint at how much she wishes she could go. Being the confident woman that she is, drenched in sexual power, guys can't help but say, "I'd be honored to take you on my arm."

Her response: "If you're expecting me to be arm candy, I don't have anything impressive to wear." Next thing you know, she has a platinum card in her hand, to buy a mega-wattage dress and shoes, an appointment at an exclusive spa to get her hair, nails and makeup done, so she can make a grand entrance – quite fortunate for someone who wants to network, since getting noticed draws people to her, of their own volition, versus her grovelling to get someone's attention, let alone an introduction.

Once you can give yourself the permission to wield your sexual power for personal gain as comfortably as this paragon, the sky's the limit with respect to what you can do with it; but using it half-heartedly will take the fun out of it, and possibly cause you to feel bad about yourself, according to Dr. Buss.

Two classic cases of women who enjoyed using their sexual power rather brazenly and comfortably, to get what they wanted are, Natalie Dylan and Stephanie Gershon.

In Natalie's case, she wanted to obtain a master's degree in family and marriage therapy, but didn't have enough money to do so. So she auctioned her virginity, partly as a fundraiser and partly as a study of women's sexual value. Within five months, ten thousand bids had been placed, with the highest bid approximating four million dollars. Naturally she made international headlines and was interviewed about her tactic. Her response, "I think me and the person I do it with both profit greatly from the deal."

As for Stephanie, she yearned to explore the Amazonian rainforest, but couldn't find a tour guide who'd take her past the edge of the forest. When she asked a busboy at a local restaurant if she could survive the rainforest on her own for two weeks, he laughed and told her she was nuts. But when he revealed that he had deep knowledge of the jungle, she turned on her charm, gave him every flirtatious signal imaginable, and got him to become her guide. She had no qualms about using her sexual magnetism to gather the following experience:

> "It was amazing. We built our homes out of palm leaves, I saw animals I'd never seen before, he taught me the medicinal properties of all the plants, we picked fruit off the trees, we swam with and ate the piranhas. And, of course, we had sex ... for almost two weeks. It was a good barter both ways. I got to stay in the jungle, and he got to have sex with a cute young American girl."

What the two stories have in common is, a sense of forthrightness, since they were both clear on what they were giving and receiving, and felt that it was fair in both directions.

This is consistent with the *Social Exchange Theory*, which stipulates that both men and women are attracted to those who can provide them with the resources they seek, in exchange for the assets they can provide. The exchange can be of any kind but it must be "fair" – i.e. both parties must believe they are acquiring the right rewards for the right price.

Sure beats unfair exchanges, especially those which are carried out underhandedly. Point being, if we decide to use our sexual power we should be honest about it, so we can ensure that it's a fair trade, satisfying all parties in one way or another. It also keeps judgements at bay, especially those that we hold against ourselves.

Speaking of fair trades – sans any judgement – Dr. Jocelyn Elders, who was a surgeon general under President Bill Clinton, agrees with what many sex trade workers say about their right to sell sexual services: it isn't any different from a brainiac selling their knowledge, an artist selling their creation, and so on. She went on record saying:

> *"We say that [hookers] are selling their bodies, but how is that different from athletes? They're selling their bodies. Models? They're selling their bodies. Actors? They're selling their bodies."*

Such a validation does make it easier for one to take their sexual power out of the closet and use it. But validation or not, this phenomenon isn't unique to North America. Anthropologist Donald Symons, author of *The Evolution of Human Sexuality* (5), studied sexual bartering and revealed that exchanges of gifts and sex occur in every culture. What's more, they often abide by the same rules, implying evolutionary benefits. A case in point: women hold greater sexual power than men, since their sexuality is something men desire and value rather highly, allowing women to be in the driver's seat when it comes to sexual economics.

Dr. Buss's research backs that up as well. He found that independent of ethnicity, socio-economic status, level of education, religion, etc., men desire sex objects, women desire success objects, for evolutionary reasons. For men, it's about spreading their seed to genetically viable and superior females; for women, to ensure pair bonding with someone of means, who can take care of them and their progeny, should that seed lead to fruition. What further intensifies this advantage is what's known as *the sexual over-perception bias* (6), defined as a generic tendency for men to over-infer a woman's sexual interest in them, based on ambiguous information; such as, a gentle touch, extended eye contact, a smile, moving into close proximity – signals which make them think a woman is sexually interested, so they become more invested. This is especially significant when the women is attractive.

Interestingly, women can spend up to 45 minutes getting to know someone – taking a keen interest in them – to see if they're worth investing in. Can you see how that adds to the confusion?

But that's not to say that it doesn't work in the other direction as well; one has to spend a mere evening in a bar to see how sexy bad boys and players have a distinct advantage – especially when it comes to sexual power – in both straight as well as gay interactions. It comes down to calling a spade and spade and being honest about it. Owning our power can also play heavily into building our self-esteem – a win-win situation.

Dr. Buss and Dr. Meston agree with the concept, "A woman's self-esteem affects, and is affected by, her sexuality, her sexual experiences, and her sex appeal."

Put another way, in Erica Jong's (7) words: *"If sex and creativity are often seen by dictators as subversive activities, it's because they lead to the knowledge that you own your own body (and with it your own voice), and that's the most revolutionary insight of all."*

Speaking of sex and creativity, how enjoyable an interaction can get will likely depend upon how a player can weave a tapestry between the two, without getting non-exploitive. I've known individuals who take their time, paying attention to every last detail, to create the perfect setup; so much so that you'll be hard-pressed to guess who's the cat and who's the mouse – it spikes the delicious cocktail of control and desire in the same vein as games where "a slave is a master in disguise," making both parties feel in charge.

The overnight success of E. L. James' *Fifty Shades of Grey* (8) is a testament to just that – the devil is definitely in the details. The character Christian Grey's take-charge nature titillated and captured tens of thousands of women, above and beyond the protagonist it was intended for, Anastasia Steele. And the playroom that could've otherwise appeared scary left many squirming over "mommy porn," contemplating kink perhaps for the very first time – truly a case of not a dry panty in the house.

Had it been bluntly introduced by a partner, it may have had quite the opposite effect. But regardless of all the delightful fun and games, since sex has a lot of power and pleasure associated with it, society has treated it as a controlled substance, by enforcing monogamy to avoid chaos.

Writer Michael B. Davie finds it interesting:

"... how societies through the ages, not just dictatorships, have always sought to control sexuality within societal constructs, including the institution of marriage that legally restricts and confines individuals and sexuality to a monogamous arrangement, whereby sex is no longer forbidden, but is limited to a single partner with the emphasis on procreation and family. And one is expected to work wage jobs for most of their life, to support this societal construct, limiting personal freedom in the process, to exist in narrow confines as a cog in the machine, as a 'productive member of society'. From the early ages of mankind, marriage has reigned in sexuality that if not controlled by society might have resulted in populations living uncontrolled lives of pleasure and individuality, along with broken families. This societal control was still very much apparent in the 1950s, especially in the TV shows, but society has become more hedonistic in recent decades."

The need to regulate sexual power only highlights how potent it is. And when you're dealing with such a potent entity, it's important to know what it's use and misuse can do, the very reason for this book, intended to release that knowledge to the masses, versus being limited to the chosen few who get to control it; or for that matter those who have the permission to use and flaunt it unapologetically.

Chapter 3

Sex Appeal – A Double Edged Sword

As a psychotherapist, I have a constant stream of women coming into my office who are unaware of their sexual power, since they hold onto the fabricated myths perpetuated by oppressive media, where sex appeal is all about numbers, quantified for easy saleability – from their age, to their weight, to measurements of different parts of their bodies. It puts some of them in a state of constant self-loathing and recrimination.

What they don't realize is that they've become paralyzed, unable to dance to their own rhythm, or notice how their captivating smiles, curves, wiggles, laughter, and various body parts – from their painted toe nails to their tousled white hair – are working their magic on those who surround them. If only they could see the likes of my friend *CoCo La Crème* bringing down the house with her luscious curves, during one of her burlesque performances!

But their fears make their world really small, where they're stuck between wanting to look their best and hating the world for making them feel that way. Over time, their repeated complaints against the supposed superficiality of sex appeal cause them to lose the magnetic pull of their own sexual power, possibly plummeting them further down a bottomless pit of low self-esteem. And they end up doing exactly what they accuse others of, i.e. judging people by their looks – particularly those whom the media promotes as beautiful and sexy – more harshly than judges they wouldn't want to face themselves. Personally, I feel the problem lies with what's constantly being endorsed by the media as the normative standard for sex appeal, when Ogi Oggas and Sai Gaddam's book *A Billion Wicked Thoughts* (9) has aptly demonstrated that the majority doesn't appear to agree with that 'standard.'

Combining online behavioral data with cutting edge neuroscience, they uncovered startling truths to make just that point, via findings which included facts like, men prefer overweight women to underweight women; men often seek erotic videos featuring women in their 50s and 60s; and so on. But since that's not what the media promotes, many women are distressed by the battle between wanting to be sexy and condoning false standards of sexiness.

Attorney and author, Tamara Shayne Kagel (10), refers to this dilemma as a state of cognitive dissonance that most women inhabit, but refuse to acknowledge. She says:

> *"We judge other women for using their looks to their advantage and attempt to course-correct their behavior by snickering behind their backs about who's had Botox injections and who still goes to a tanning salon. But these same women – myself included – take time every day to put on mascara and concealer and occasionally even fake eye lashes."*

Talk about mixed messages which confuse even the most cerebral of feminists. At the opposite end of the spectrum are those who see their sexual power at work, but then complain that they're being objectified. Thankfully, activist Mira Veda (11) has put that way of thinking into perspective. She says:

"In general, objectification and sexualisation seem to be two widely misunderstood concepts. Objectification is when someone is turned into a purely sexual object and deprived of all humanity. The object is stripped of any agency and denied any power. Sexualisation is often conflated with the influence of negative media imagery, rarely taking into account sexual empowerment and agency."

Given that distinction, it goes to reason then, if one is wielding their sexual power willingly, it needn't be labelled as objectification.

Perhaps self-objectification can be considered a class unto itself, as portrayed by feminist pop artists who feel sexually empowered when they entertain the crowds by moving in sexually provocative ways – seen by some as degrading. The phenomenon has lent itself to the question, "Can a woman simultaneously objectify herself and be a symbol of female empowerment?"

Beyoncé, the most powerful woman in show biz believes that it's indeed possible. A self-professed feminist, she crawled on all fours at an

MTV Video Awards ceremony, while maintaining her feminist stance. It caused a huge reaction.

Madiha Bhatti, a feminist poet, who believes that celebrities should be held accountable for such behaviours, since they are role models who impact the young in profound ways, was quite disturbed by the performance. Her compelling, video-taped poem in response to it went viral in record time.

One is left wondering, how can two strongly feminist women strongly disagree on what sexual empowerment means?"

Elizabeth Plank, senior editor at Mic news, put it into perspective in her brilliant article on the phenomenon (12):

> *"So, ultimately, is the problem that Beyoncé performs "on all fours," as Bhatti notes in her poem, or that we assume certain things about women on all fours. Moreover, what if Beyoncé wants to crawl on all fours? The problem isn't self-objectification, it's the sexism that puts down women who engage in it ... Although award shows usually make feminists cringe, this year's [2014] VMAs gave us hope. And it wasn't just Beyoncé ... so much so that New York magazine is (ironically) asking if there was a feminist conspiracy. As Eliana Dockterman at TIME points out, 'This year's VMAs were all about empowered women,' a far cry from last year's Robin*

Thicke and Miley Cyrus creeptastic performance that had us talking about the lack of role models for young teenagers watching.

... So can female artists proudly identify as feminists while taking pleasure in self-objectification? Perhaps the answer lies somewhere between Beyoncé's affinity for pantless outfits and her penchant for penning essays about gender equality. Maybe the modern woman shouldn't have to choose."

I for one couldn't agree more – why choose when you can have it all?

Another example of media controversy, which misses this point is the recent outrage over artist Milo Manara's cover for the first issue of *Marvel*'s new *Spider-Woman* series, because *Spider-Woman*'s rear is submissively hoisted in the air in Nicki Minaj type fashion. But the artist and many others believe that since she's featured as a strong female character – versus a helpless one, in a flimsy plot line no less – she can wear whatever the heck she pleases. She's comfortable with her sexuality ... and just plain comfortable – would you wanna fight crime wearing something cumbersome? And she isn't portrayed any differently from male super-heroes – gay or straight.

Isn't it high time that we acknowledge that sexual power doesn't make one powerless in other areas, like repelling magnetic polarity? In fact, it's wired into our primal instincts to enhance other forms of power. As such, it shouldn't be downplayed for its lack of "political correctness."

The movie *Six Days Seven Nights* captures the confusion around such mixed messages rather well: Anne Heche is seen in tight shorts with Harrison Ford's gaze glued to her derriere, ready to follow her into dangerous waters. As if she has eyes in the back of her head, she reprimands him for staring at her butt; to which he responds, "I'm sure when you went to buy those shorts you asked the salesperson for something really ugly that no one would ever look at." Point being, if you got it and you wanna flaunt it, do it with pride, not shame, which disempowers you to your own detriment.

That said, that can only happen if we shed the negative labels which don't serve us anymore. In a culture where men's physical power is compared to women's sexual power, degrading the latter while upholding the former is nothing short of sexism.

But society tends to feel more comfortable oppressing those who own their sexual power and wear it with great pride. Even officers of the law can fall prey to that, instead of guarding and protecting it.

A case in point: a Toronto police officer was speaking to the female students at a university campus, alerting them to a serial rapist. Without a moment of hesitation, he advised that they not "dress like sluts" for their own safety, as if dressing a certain way – or for that matter, owning their sexual power – was an invitation for sexual assault. Thankfully, that marked the beginning of the annual "Slut Walk", where millions of women march the world over, to protect their right to dress any way they desire, and to remove the pejorative meaning of the word "slut." How exciting is that?

A while back, I too was honoured with the task of liberating another pejorative word – "cunt" – from the derogatory meaning that's generally implied by its use, and returning the power to it that it so deserves.

I was delivering one of Eve Ensler's *Vagina Monologues* (13) at *Second City* dinner theater for V Day, to raise funds for a women's shelter. My piece "Reclaiming Cunt" was particularly challenging, since I had to elevate the audience's emotions from a tragic place to a celebratory place, to create a smooth transition from sad dialogues to pleasurable dialogues. So I decided to go center stage and own it. By the end of the piece, I had the audience spell out the word C.U.N.T. by leading a cheer, as I bounced around like a cheerleader.

On one side of me was Cindy Williams, the star of the seventies sitcom *Laverne and Shirley*; on the other side, the illustrious Joyce Dewitt, the star of *Three's Company*, another sitcom from the seventies. Not sure who had a bigger reaction – Cindy with a dropped jaw, or Joyce with an ear to ear grin. Either way, it was a clear example of how differently we react, when it comes to flaunting the power behind a sexual word.

So, why exactly is sexual power sometimes seen so differently, by different people, at different times, making it a double edged sword? Because despite its numerous benefits, when women wield it they are shamed and slighted – and often labelled as immoral – even where men may be edified for the same behaviours, under the same circumstances.

Thankfully, females like Beyoncé, the cast of *Girls*, and the character Kalinda Sharma on *The Good Wife* are quite comfortable using their sexual power, while acknowledging that with such great power comes great responsibility – which cannot be embraced if we can't embrace the power itself!

And as far as power goes, there isn't another greater power that's created greater controversy. For example, the contentious "pornography wars" at the dawn of the feminist era, involving uncompromising feminists like Susan Brownmiller, who were passionately opposed to porn; versus feminists like Candida Royalle, who felt that if feminism is about freeing women, then they should be allowed to look at or appear in porn, wielding their sexual power any way they want.

Ultimately, it comes down to freedom of choice, allowing one to be a gatekeeper of their own center, be that as a Diva in any shape, form, or hue – wearing a kickass dress and high heels if she chooses – who can make men chase their tails like a dog; or a feminist like Erica Jong, who believes that "Sexual freedom can be a smoke-screen for how far we haven't come."

That said, even freedom means different things to different people, not unlike sexual power – it's all about the lens that each is viewed through, making it feel good or bad. Either way, no one can argue with the power itself, whether it's seen as taken, given, or used – with a knee-jerk mindset no less – depending upon whether women are seen as things to be consumed, or consumers who can be defiant and dodge the discourse of shame.

If you can do the latter, more power to you!

Why not embrace the BITCH inside you – i.e. **B**abe **I**n **T**otal **C**ontrol of **H**erself – and have fun with her! Comedian Jocelyn (14) says:

"Your Inner Bitch is not rude, or cruel at all. She is the antithesis of being a self-sacrificing doormat. Practicing this Art is about feeling in control of your experience, rooted in self-respect; knowing what you want and being unwilling to compromise your standards.

Jocelyn believes in dancing with that inner bitch, while accepting the dark side that lives within her.

Mama Gena, author of *Using the Power of Pleasure to Have Your Way with the World*, (15), and owner of the *School of Womanly Arts,* dedicated to "teaching women how to use the power of pleasure to have their way with the world", elaborates on why that's important. She says, 'The only way your dark side can work against you is if you don't own it."

Jocelyn goes onto say that that's very true, because ...

"... if you don't own your darkness, that means either you deny it and don't even recognize it exists, or you know that she is there but you are constantly pushing her aside and telling her to shut up. That's very destructive, because that means that there is a large part of you who is not getting her needs met.

In light of that, why exactly might a woman deny her delicious "dark side"? Because she starts getting brainwashed very early on.

If you find yourself wondering why the life that you're living feels like someone else's life, it may well be because you're living the life that has been dictated to you by your family, culture and society. And even though your natural instincts may have been choked by them, you don't know any better, because you've been so immersed in the milieu. But if your best friend were to be experiencing the same suffocation – worse, stuck in an abusive situation – you'd find it to be egregious and ask her to leave the situation that's killing her lifeblood immediately.

It's analogous to what happens to a frog. If it's placed in a pot of water which is set to boil, it'll just stay there, even as it's boiling, since it continues to adapt to its life-threatening environment; but if you were to try to put it into boiling water from the outside, it would recognize the danger and not go anywhere near it.

It's time we took a step outside ourselves and our environment to take a good look at whether our life feels magical or unfulfilled. Beyond that, we should fight the very cultural constraints which bind us into looking a certain way, or feeling shame when we embrace our inner desires and instincts.

If Barbie were real, she couldn't walk, she'd have to crawl, thanks to her proportions. Yet, that's one of the first symbols we present to little girls – a standard they might aspire to one day. Small wonder eating disorders are devouring more and more girls, at younger and younger ages. And if that isn't bad enough, they're also being bombarded by fairy tales where females wait to be rescued by Prince Charming; later, literature that pushes female coyness.

Sadly, all of that causes women to become disconnected from what they find desirable, in favor of what they *think* they should find to be desirable, making it challenging for them to enjoy their sexuality and the sexual power that goes with it.

Anthropologist Helen Fischer, author of *Why We Love* (16), has done extensive research into the human sexual make-up. She says, "Being a human who is sexual, who is allowed to be sexual, is a freedom accorded by society much more readily to males than to females." How sad is that?

Thankfully, scientific research is challenging those notions and giving women the permission to be sexually authentic, versus moulding themselves in artificial ways, just to cope with the cognitive dissonance.

In his book *What Do Women Want? Adventures in the Science of Female Desire* (17), author Daniel Bergner delves into those very studies in female sexuality, particularly lust – i.e. what turns women on and how. From monogamy killing women's libidos to women being turned on by being desired/objectified, females are acknowledged as sexually aggressive, not passive – as they've been portrayed in the past, waiting to be pursued.

Dorothy Black (18), who studies female sexuality, comments on these findings as follows:

"Turns out, the story that's been packaged and sold to us about our bodies, desires and sex drive – as fact – might have been more than just a little bit influenced by that creepy old man in the corner called patriarchy.

This is nothing new to subcultures that still venerate and nurture female sexual energy as a force to be reckoned with. My first experience of this was with Shakti Malan, a now world-renowned tantrika who runs workshops showing women how to tap into their desire and 'drop into' their own bodies.

If you're wondering what other bodies we've collectively dropped into, just open any women's glossy and take a look at what your sexual power is being sold to you as: demure, made-up, withholding, brittle with frailty and in stasis, waiting to satisfy The One."

Denying those false and/or controversial messages, and embracing what is, is the spirit in which sexual power must manifest itself, with a heart and soul which knows what it wants and is willing to dance to its own rhythm to get it, with neither side of the great divide telling it what it must do.

And it needs to happen with eyes wide open.

Chapter 4

Sexual Power in Relationships

Being a sex therapist, I have a front row seat to the sexual dynamics in myriad relationships, each one more complicated than the next. But one thing they all have in common is, just as the person who loves less has greater power in the relationship, the person with lower desire has greater sexual power in a relationship, because they get to control the couple's sex life, for the most part.

It's clearly obvious in session, whether it's playing out in front of me, or shamefully trying to hide behind my analyst's couch – as is often the case when one stays and stays and stays in an abusive and disastrous relationship, because they're hooked on off-the-charts sex and chemistry like crack cocaine. From tallies to barters, sex can indeed become coinage for reward and punishment in couples with mismatched libidos, which is a lot more common than you might realize – one in three couples to be exact. Beyond that, sex can also become the focus of power plays, when one's ego gets wrapped up in it. Either way, its ripple effect extends forever, in a highly convoluted manner, since it impacts the psyche in astronomical ways, as we identify with our sexuality and all that emanates from it.

A sexual woman who tries to initiate things with her male partner, only to not get taken seriously – or worse, get turned down time and again due to his machismo reasons – will eventually stop initiating. If the rejection makes her question her sex appeal, she may then seek outside validation. If she's pissed off at losing her sexual power with her partner, she may try to even the odds by using it to get what she wants, when she wants it, wherever she can get it.

Another example of this ripple effect can go as follows: John – a fictitious, composite character – has a higher libido than his wife, so he comes up with creative ways to sexually engage her more often than she'd like, using everything from his charm, to backrubs, to candlelit dinners, to entice her. At first, he feels he has the power to seduce like Casanova. But with time, he realizes that's not the case; his pleas for touch fall on deaf ears, because she'll be intimate with him only when *she* feels like it.

Seduction may change into begging at that point, and eventually arguments, making him look less and less attractive to her. And if that isn't enough of a beating for his sagging ego, the sting of constant rejection is sure to get him.

Ultimately, John will feel powerless and thus stop making advances altogether, which is bound to make him feel unhappy, and possibly angry, resulting in the disintegration of his sexually diminished relationship. At that point, if John finds attention elsewhere, he'd likely be too vulnerable to resist.

When we fall in love, it's very much a mirror-mirror-on-the-wall situation, since our amour reflects back only the good in us, making us feel like we're the fairest of all. But when that stops – i.e. our partner starts to reflect our bad parts and ignore the good parts – the proverbial mirror is shattered, bringing bad luck to the relationship. John may thus decide to have an affair, out of a "sense of entitlement" contradictory as it may be to his marital vows – most affairs start when someone stops feeling special at home and someone outside the home makes them the centre of their world.

The affair, in turn, will cause a shift in relationship power, because not too many things can match the pain of a betrayal, other than possibly the pain of rejection, as the following story captures ever so eloquently and painfully: Librarian Chuck Fisher, who always finds himself waiting for his partner in anticipation, hoping she'll take mercy on him, says a quote from Ravi Zacharias' Book, *Can Man Live Without God* (19), relates to him in that context:

> *"On one occasion, it was narrated that Joseph Stalin called for a live chicken and proceeded to use it to make an unforgettable point before some of his henchmen. Forcefully clutching the chicken in one hand, he began to systematically pluck out its feathers with the other hand. As the chicken struggled in vain to escape, he continued with the painful denuding until the bird was completely stripped. 'Now you watch,' Stalin said as he placed the chicken on the floor and walked away with some bread crumbs in his hand. Incredibly, the fear-crazed chicken hobbled toward him and clung to the legs of his trousers. Stalin threw a handful to the bird, and it began to follow him around the room. Stalin turned to his dumbfounded colleagues and said quietly, 'This is the*

> *way to rule the people. Did you see how that chicken followed me for food, even though I had caused it such torture? People are like that chicken. If you inflict inordinate pain on them they will follow you for food the rest of their lives.'"*

As Fisher observes:

> *"In a sexless marriage, you don't cuddle with your soul-mate, you cling to your jailer. You don't thank God every morning for the pain, you wonder if today will be the day that some semblance of mercy will be extended to you. You don't share great moments with your life partner, you pray that God will enable your children to escape your fate."*

Now, if that doesn't describe the sexual power behind the "yes" versus "no" – in a dance between excruciating pain and pleasure – not much else could. And this power play often gets established long before the "I do's" – when one is merely hoping to date someone, for instance. It's like the chicken or the egg – if we are to stick with chicken analogies – as in, is it that he/she who holds the cards on the if's and when's of dating and sex has the power, or does the power get *established* when one holds on dearly to those cards in the first place?

Margaret Mitchell opens up *Gone with the Wind*, with – "Scarlett O'Hara was not beautiful, but men seldom realized it when caught by her charm." And what charm she had, giving her the power to pick and choose from men sitting at her feet, hoping to get selected by her for a mere dance. By definition, the word charm refers to the [sexual] power of pleasuring or attracting; and it implies magic, because it doesn't make any sense a lot of times. And so it was with Scarlett and many men and women today, who have sexual power, and the magic that goes along with it, to have people swooning.

Beyond that, a woman with sexual power sees herself as more than a mere half of any duality – even when she's in a relationship – because she typically has more done for her than she's willing to do; not because she's lazy, but because she loves the power and the freedom to do what she really needs and likes to do. And she exercises that power in a way that makes her pursuers value her all the more, because she values herself first and foremost, even as she captivates others.

She thinks big, so she *is* big! In relationships, she gets to call the shots, instead of wondering what she did wrong and apologizing when her partner is at fault. In fact, she apologizes for little, least of all for using her sexual power, be it for the sheer purpose of satisfying her lust, or for other personal gains.

A woman with sexual power is courageous and often outrageous, and confident enough to want to share the secret to her self-assuredness with other women. In a world where females can loathe captivating women and underhandedly cut each other, she passionately converts them to her way of thinking – seen by her as a better way for the sisterhood – one woman at a time.

Why is she so generous? Because she feels there's enough fun to be had by everyone, in any size, form, shape, ethnicity, or orientation, so she doesn't believe in containing sexual power, where it could become stifled, or lose its magnetic charge – the very reason she has irresistible gravitational pull! Is she a stick figure? Not likely, as most won't see her as sexy in that case, making her job all the more challenging.

Cynthia Heimel, author of *Advanced Sex Tips for Girls* (20), believes that the skinny on being skinny:

> *"... may be a giant conspiracy amongst fashion editors to propagandize everyone into becoming so bony that they can't get laid, and who will therefore spend more time looking at ads for mascara that will allegedly help them get laid."*

I for one know how alluring those mascara ads can be; I used to have duplicates of wands that didn't work in the first place, because I didn't want my peepers to miss out on the promise of "lashing out."

Now I know better, because ultimately sexual power is a potent cocktail of attitude, owning and working what you got, and not being afraid of letting your sexuality emanate like the scent of your pheromones. And if you happen to feel good enough to rock a hot outfit with stockings and stilettos – regardless of your age or shape – or wear red lipstick brazenly, all the better. But only for your own sake, not because you feel pressured – that would be at a cost to your authenticity, which puts the power in someone else's hands.

Chapter 5

Self Esteem – Sexual Empowerment and Disempowerment

I felt ugly as I was growing up, and felt I didn't belong in a family of beautiful people. *The Ugly Duckling* thereby became my favorite storybook. So while all the other girls were playing pretty, reading about their Prince Charming rescuing them, I was hoping that my family of swans would find me so I could rescue myself.

And then it happened. I reached puberty at age nine – 36 C breasts, major curves and aunt flow – truly the whole nine yards in my case. Suddenly I was the center of attention – all the boys (plus my male teachers) started to notice me, wanted to hang around me and do favours for me.

I can't tell you how many times I was offered everything from their mom's jewelry to a blingy hunk of chandelier, flowers, poetry, carrying of my books, and all other manner of romantic folklore. But I couldn't accept, because I wasn't raised to revel in my power. I was raised to feel shame for "luring" everyone – as if I were Jezebel, even though I didn't know about her at the time.

So, my non-existent self-esteem plummeted below ground level, pushing my negative feelings about myself underground.

Dr. Steve Howard, in *Brazen Femme* (21), refers to shame as the "... unseen engine that drives a lot of other unpleasant, self-defeating, negative feelings and behaviours ... the operative emotion behind self-criticism, low self-esteem, envy and depression."

With time, I realized that maybe the huge breasts – now a G cup – which lay on my chest like an S on Superman's chest had some super power stored in them after all, which hypnotized and mesmerized the eyes fixated upon them. I even went as far as asking my physics teacher if I had spinach stuck between my boobs, when his gaze was shamelessly fixed upon them.

But alas, my new found sense of power was to be crushed yet again, when my mother insisted upon changing the way I dressed, to avoid "unwanted" attention. I obliged, even though everything inside me was screaming, *but I want the attention ... I like it ... please don't take it away from me ... I've finally started to feel good about myself!*

Connecting my self-esteem to my body and outside validation came so naturally to me – something that all other self-loathing females confess to struggling with every day.

*   *   *

Fast forward to us moving to Canada; I became an outcast once again. But this time we were too far away for the swans in India to find me – my swansong was over, my fate now locked into a powerless existence of racism and bullying. Then one day, while working at the *Golden Arches*, I went to a staff picnic. All we had to bring was shorts and T shirts – everything else would be provided for us. Out came my long legs, while my breasts strained to break free out of a tight T shirt, borrowed from my B-cup cousin with tea-cup breasts. Everyone was shocked and asked me where I'd been hiding that bod all this time?

It was a eureka moment – I started to sneak a pair of shorts and a T shirt to school every day, so maybe the waves of negative attention would change their course to positive attention. It worked like a charm. Instead of being stuffed down a garbage can by the jocks, I was invited to join the cheerleading team; instead of being ignored by the cool kids, the coolest guy in the school suddenly wanted to date me.

I didn't know at the time that it was all about sexual power. But my self-esteem was starting to surface above ground. Once again, the flowers, offers to have my books carried for me, and so on, resurfaced along with it. Being content with that, I didn't do much to harness that power and use it wisely. Truth be told, I didn't even know what it was until that cold winter night outside of the uber hot and happening club in the Big Apple. Now that I recognize sexual power for what it is, I smile every time I see a woman blossom because of it, particularly one who's able to beat the horrible odds that life dished her way.

A case in point: my friend – let's call her Jane – who's fifty, doesn't have a cover-girl face or body, yet, she's the most sexually powerful woman I know, who can date anyone she pleases. Whether she's in a relationship or flying solo, whenever she walks into a room, she has a huge presence – people stop and take notice. They're mesmerized by her sexual aura and will do anything she asks of them. It's her smile, the bounce in her walk, her flirtatious eyes which make you wonder what she's thinking, and a tilt in her chin that says "I like you, anything's possible."

Another example, my friend Terri-Jean Bedford, author of *Dominatrix on Trial* (22), is a Professional Dominatrix who makes a living wielding her sexual power like a whip. It's electric, it's the ultimate power play, it's sexy – so much so that men go to extremes to experience it, and are willing to surrender their own power to it. Even chatting with her is quite the experience, watching the confidence which stems from her persona and a lifetime of sexual power and power plays, that made it possible for her to turn around her tough life, which began in poverty and discrimination. And she continues to use that power to effect major change, successfully lobbying for sex workers who are victims of abuse due to archaic laws.

And then there's Sarah Symonds, author of *Having an Affair? A Handbook for the Other Woman* (23), a self-professed "infidelity expert" who discusses the use of sexual power in obtaining fame and fortune, based in her own experiences as Lord Archer's and Gordon Ramsey's ex-mistress – two extremely powerful men brought to their knees by her super powers. But she's very adamant that one has to be clear on what they're getting in exchange for their sexual power, versus having delusions around something more than a clear-cut barter – something we alluded to earlier on.

Now while I'm not condoning Sarah's actions in any way, especially since they involve robbing other women's stables, I have to wonder why those who reprimanded her didn't do the same with the men involved – after all, *they* were the married ones, not her. Could it be that forgiving men for succumbing to sexual power ties into their hard-wiring to blindly give into it, providing an equalizing force for women?

Regardless, women who use that power are often referred to as whores, and put down for playing up the pleasurable part of sex. According to Dr. Betty Dodson, the "Godmother of Masturbation" in her forward to Inga Muscio's book *Cunt* (24):

> *"If they [women] celebrate sexual pleasure they will be attacked by right-wing factions. ... Until more feminists have the courage to openly claim and enjoy their own sexuality and sexual pleasure, the women's movement will remain stuck in joyless discourse which does not improve society.*
>
> *I've been told by corporate feminists that talking about sexual pleasure when there is so much sexual violence against women is inappropriate, insensitive and politically incorrect."*

Dodson compares that to giving up food because there's so much violence caused by hunger, among other things. Point being, we should be allowed to choose what we want to do with our sexual desire and power. Which is not to say that I'm being insensitive to the sexual trauma endured by one in four women – I see the trappings every day and help women work through them. But once our work is done I want them to be able to enjoy healthy sexuality, instead of fearing that that would imply they're condoning what they've endured – even though the two have nothing to do with each other – a far cry from it! I strongly believe that the reward for their tough healing journey should be sexual freedom, among other things.

But whether or not a woman has gone through the heartache of sexual trauma, she has every right to feel worthy of enjoying her sexual self – be it in the form of her erotic lust, sexual power, or the dance of intimacy – no one else has the right to take that away from her. The people who try to do so are equally responsible for ravaging her, be they those who inflict trauma, or those who make her feel like a whore for enjoying her gifts – destroying her freedom in the name of freedom – to me they're both guilty of victimizing her.

When people wield other forms of power, they don't feel shame, they don't make excuses, they don't do it half-heartedly – in fact, they do so with great pride – so why should sexual power be any different?

*　　　*　　　*

I've learned long since my own days of breaking through the *self*-esteem barrier that the focus of one's *self*-esteem should be within one*self*, but if outside forces add to someone feeling better about themselves then far be it for me to stop them. After all, it began that way for me as well.

But the danger lies in the focus *remaining* outside, once you taste what a strong sense of self can do. While the objects of your desire and sexual power can indeed exist outside of you, the engine which fuels those forces should be within you – non-reliant on outside validation to feed itself, because that would defy the whole purpose. Isn't it high time that we put the "*self*" back into the heart of *self*-esteem?

At the end of the day it's about us enjoying a force which equalizes against all else. But in order for us to enjoy that force, we need to accept ourselves wholly and wholeheartedly!

Toward that end, Sex Therapist Alexandra Katehakis, author of *Erotic Intelligence: Igniting Hot, Healthy Sex While in Recovery from Sex Addiction* (25), wrote in a piece on Body Image, for the Center for Healthy Sex:

> *"Bodily ideals, although diverging wildly in different cultures and periods, challenge and judge every individual – even the seemingly 'beautiful'. While such aesthetic standards can encourage healthy self-improvement, they often impair self-acceptance. We have constant proof of our corporeal failings – and of our inevitably temporary and comparative successes. An exalted, unrealistic sense of one's bodily perfection cannot substitute for a*

realistic, healthy body image. ... We're all built into bodies that have innumerable socially unacceptable realities like susceptibility to illness, elimination, and deterioration, to name only a few. To deny any aspect of your actual body and functions is to cut yourself off from life and reality. ... How can you separate your identity from your body, and show your body as much kindness and compassion as you might show an honored guest? If you aim to grow your psychological capacity for healthy relationships, learning to love your body unconditionally is a good place to start – after all, you're rather attached to it!"

If we don't love and enjoy our bodies, we can't possibly love and enjoy the sexual power they emanate. But if we can embrace every last bit of ourselves, we can generate the most powerful form of sexual energy, which can propel us wherever we want to go. Author, Mistress Singing Deer, expressed this well in *Brazen Femme* (21):

"When we lock away parts of ourselves we believe to be shameful, unacceptable or unlovable based on the messages we get from the world around us, we become fractured, split. When those 'unlovable' parts remain hidden away in the shadows, we are not whole, and if we deny the complexity of what we are, we're walking around with only a portion of our power. We're not all that we can be in the world."

Chapter 6
Sex, Lies, and Video Takes
The Use of Sex Appeal in the Media

I often find myself breathless, with a pounding heart, white-knuckled around my *Diet Coke*, as I witness a familiar scenario – different drama series, different players, but the same sequence. Their eyes meet, words are barely exchanged, and next thing you know they're ravishing each other with urgency, against a wall/door, atop a desk/counter, gyrating together flawlessly with perfectly choreographed moves – with the flexibility of gymnasts no less – until they coalesce into a hot and sweaty simultaneous orgasm, and then melt into each other's arms, spent and satiated.

It makes me feel like I'm missing something in my relationship – that tsunami of passionate pleasure, drenched with slick wet juices – even though I should know better, since I work in the media and am privy to all that goes into every perfect second of a production.

It must be because my otherwise cerebral brain gets hijacked to its reptilian side, since that visceral thinking then extends into the commercials – seeing perfectly chosen and staged lingerie models strut their stuff, I find myself thinking *if I had that bod I'd love to strut it around on the beach.*

But once I imagine those stilettos digging into sand, I snap back into reality and realize my life's better than fantasy, because I do have an intensely satisfying relationship that outlasts the fifty minute hour. And if I were to own my body with pride I could also turn heads, as I already have, on quite a few occasions – like the voluptuous women at *Caribana* parades who own their bodies, and sway this way and that, looking sexier and more captivating than any celluloid beauty.

A case in point: I once accompanied my friend David Menzies, columnist for major publications, to the Toronto Auto Show, to comment on the sex appeal of various cars and trucks. I had my "power suit" on – i.e. tight black leggings and matching top with thigh-high red boots – and managed to turn quite a few heads. I walked around as if I owned the place, since Menzies had arranged for a special media pass to photograph me near cars that cost more than the average home. Watching everyone's reaction, he said, "I just went from feeling like a big shot for having you with me, to wanting to *be* you, so I can experience your sexual power."

A few weeks later, he asked if I'd be a *"Bud Girl"* for an article he was writing about *Super Bowl* parties. All I'd have to do was don a *Budweiser* string bikini and parade around with drinks, like a "Bevy Bim", while he interviewed men about their male-bonding ritual. FYI, these were men my age, with adult kids, so it wasn't about feeling like prey to older men, or for that matter playing a cougar preying on younger men. Regardless, I turned him down, because it felt more like objectification versus sexualisation, because I saw no personal benefit to me being staged for men or media, and because I didn't want to embarrass my own adult sons. But it felt nice being asked all the same, especially since I'm my own gatekeeper when it comes to how I use my sexual power.

In any case, I'd be reticent if I didn't highlight the fact that, all that provocative staging is mild stuff, compared to the impact of an even bigger force – a multi-billion-dollar male-focussed porn industry that's transforming how impressionable and not-so-impressionable minds look at sex, by literally changing the wiring in their brains.

It's shaping – distorting, if we're to be truly honest – the way most consumers view their relationships, because they actually believe that what they see in those movies is real, and the normative standard, i.e., ever-willing, caricaturized bodies, ready to contort every which way, to make sexualisation of their various orifices feasible, without ever demanding anything in return. Talk about raising the bar to an impossible, unreachable pinnacle, making consumers feel that their own sex lives are deficient by comparison.

In Sweden, educators are well aware of the effect of the digital world, so they've taken an unusual approach to tackle all aspects thereof – including the impact of porn on sexual perceptions – by actively bringing it into the classroom. Teachers dissect clips from pornography and invite students to discuss questions such as: "Do you think this is what a normal woman/man's body looks like?" and "Do you think the woman is enjoying this?"

Unfortunately, for North American classrooms, the Swedish way of directly addressing issues people face in this day and age, seems light years away.

As such, the impact of the erroneous messages continues to hound relationships at multiple levels, including the fact that a partner of someone who's hooked on porn often stops getting a rise out of them, thereby making them lose their sexual power in the relationship.

That said, even the consumers themselves don't have the power, since it lies with the corporations which manipulate their primal instincts. The only other entities which benefit from that are big pharma and cosmetic enhancement industries. The former, due to a boost in sales of meds which treat erectile dysfunction – impacting more and more young men, secondary to porn use – the latter, because now more than ever, both men and women are trying to emulate the look of those stars, after tirelessly fighting with their own appearance.

The irony? Sex appeal starts from within and then dances with whatever comes in its path, including the body it resides in. Having a cosmetically enhanced porn star body won't do it in and of itself, regardless of what the media preaches, to proselytize the masses to their unrelenting religion.

A new genre of "Femme Porn" is very mindful of that. Basically, it's porn for women by women, showing real fun, sans any derogatory "money shots". With more and more women consuming erotic movies, it has given them an opportunity to choose femme focussed materials, involving empowered women.

Feeling the sexual power that resides within us, embracing the body which contains it, and then dressing up that body in ways that emanate what one's feeling inside is where the magic lies.

Charlize Theron, the 39-year-old Oscar-winning actress, told *Women's Wear Daily*, at a fashion show in Paris: "I think that women find their strength and power in their sexuality, in their sensuality within, [through] getting older and being secure within that," when asked to describe womanhood.

That said, while appreciating the fact that it starts within, Theron also admires the use of sexy packaging. She gets loads of free garments from the fashion industry, giving her "a really nice closet," which she and her girlfriends call "Narnia" – perhaps for its transformative impact? Theron admits to giving some of those sensual pieces to her girlfriends, because, "I'm always very aware that I'm one person and I can't wear everything. ... My whole concept in life is if you're not using it, you should give it to somebody else so they can use it." – spoken like a true sisterhood veteran who believes in nurturing other women's sexual power, versus hoarding it for herself, like an insecure creature.

However, the advertising media loves those insecure creatures, since the media can tap into their instincts and use sex appeal to sell them just about anything; that is contingent upon making them feel defective first and foremost, so they'll blindly follow the path that leads to utopia, based on promises of reaching the zenith of their sexual power.

But what exactly does sexy look like? And are we willing to allow the media to dictate a specific standard to us, when we know that it comes from within, in *various* unique forms.

Malcom Gladwell discuses "thin slicing" in his book *Blink: The Power of Thinking Without*

Thinking (26) – a phenomenon which explains how we can be brainwashed into making snap decisions, which we may not necessarily agree with, based on constant and consistent messages and stereotypes, which invade our psyche day in and day out.

It goes to reason then, we need to find our own center, and nourish it with our own positive, powerful and transformative messages – the goal of the second half of this book – so we can enjoy the equalizing force of sexual power.

*   *   *

On the flipside of the sizzling sensuality that we're made to yearn for are messages which tell us to save our virtue. And if we happen to defy them, we're shamed for being overtly sexual. Sexual Healer Suzanne Blackburn, who is troubled by those perplexing messages, comments in "Reclaiming Eros" – *Brazen Femme* (21):

> *"Our culture sends confusing and contradictory messages about sexuality – one moment using sexy bodies to sell everything from bath soap to automobiles, the next moment telling us to abstain from sex to protect our health and virtue. ... The crassness, prevalence, and hypocrisy of these messages constitutes yet another abuse of our sexual nature."*

Beyond that, those double messages extend to sexism. While Janet Jackson was reprimanded for a somewhat expected "wardrobe malfunction" during a Super Bowl performance, Justin Timberlake wasn't expected to do any such thing, nor did he have any repercussions for tearing her outfit. And while Miley Cyrus was slammed for her animalistic moves, Robin Thicke got away with acting like an "old married pervert."

But that's all fake power, staged to perfection, because too often those whom we applaud as sex symbols are nothing more than empty cymbals, clanging away to perfectly choreographed moves, feeling like imposters in the roles they play, since what they feel inside is truly inconsistent.

Take Jessica Alba for instance – a woman known for her sexy screen roles and status as one of the world's most desirable women, who says that she's a "prude" in real life, and very different from the sex symbol label that's been attached to her. She says that many times she found that label to be confusing. Alba told *Entertainment Weekly* magazine, "I grew up Catholic. In my head I'm always thinking, "Oh God, can my grandma see this?"

When real sexual power is at work, there's nothing fake or confusing about it. It can be subtle, mysterious, and omnipotent; and it creates a level playing field, giving the otherwise disempowered, disfranchised and marginalized individuals an upper hand.

For example, in a world where women are generally paid less than men for the same job, modelling and porn industries pay women significantly more for their sex appeal than their male counterparts. There isn't a greater equalizing force than our sexuality that lives within us – we just need to connect with it, and use it ethically.

Chapter 7

Sex Addiction
Emotional Slavery to Sexual Power

Scientific research has shown that when the brain is overwhelmed with fear, trauma, or violence cues, arousal is often an automated response – it might be the brain's way of hijacking the mind to a more pleasant place.

When a child is forced to remain in those negative states for long periods of time, arousal becomes their "go to" response whenever they're distressed – a coping mechanism of sorts – because neurons which fire together wire together. And if this pairing between sex and certain emotions happens through a critical imprinting stage – i.e. first sexual feeling/experience – the brain can be fooled into thinking that you can't have one without the other, which gets hard-wired into the individual's erotic template.

In a recent study by neurobiologist Jim Pfaus (27), half of the male rats who were to mate for the very first time were made to wear little leather jackets, while the other half went sans. Both groups mated successfully. Next time they were allowed to mate again, all of them went sans. Well guess what: the ones who wore jackets the first time couldn't have sex without them – most were confused and eventually became disinterested; and those who were somewhat interested couldn't get erect. The experiment was then repeated with female rats being sprayed with the scent of death – something that rats avoid at all costs – the first time they mated. Regardless, the male rats had no problem being drawn to the females and had a jolly good time. Next time they were to mate again, the females went sans the scent, making it an ideal situation, one would think; but the male rats lost all interest in mating when they got within sniffing distance – even though they raced into the cage quite excitedly at get go, proving that their minds had been wired into fetishistic thinking.

I know we're a lot more evolved than rats – even cute little leather-clad rodents – but the wiring for our primal instincts isn't all that different; our automated thinking can take some pretty big risks when it comes to sex, if our mind makes a connection. And that right there is the basis of a sex addiction – it isn't about quantity and it doesn't make much sense when you look at the risks involved, but addicts grow up in neglectful and abusive environments, so sex becomes a soothing mechanism, which gets hard-wired when they're quite young.

As such, a sex addict can become an emotional slave to sex, where things end up being completely out of their control, and the power ends up in the hands of whosoever is feeding their sexual, self-medicating behaviour patterns, just like drug or alcohol addiction. Sexual slavery is infinitely easier to propagate, thanks to the Internet and mavens who know how to manipulate it to their advantage.

One has to barely scan how agencies like *Ashley Madison* work – an adultery website for married people, which equates monogamy with monotony – and the solicitous pop-ups from porn sites, which tempt consumers with increasingly high stakes products, playing into their novelty-seeking libidos, knowingly taking advantage of the fact that the brain easily habituates to the same old same old.

But when we're dealing with an illness – or the distressed and the depressed – the use of sexual power on the vulnerable, even when they "consent" to it, is essentially the equivalent of statutory rape.

Sadly, there are many unethical individuals and companies that don't know when to stop – or simply don't care – and skillfully feed off enslaving the vulnerable masses. They first create the hunger and then hold satiety hostage, so the victims are willing to give up anything for it – much like Esau signing away his birthright to Jacob, when his severe, primal hunger for food made him act insanely.

It goes back to using sexual power ethically and responsibly, which is why those who evaluate the barter and forge ahead in ethical ways should feel comfortable with it, versus those who use it underhandedly. But society punishes the former and applauds the latter. It's as if wearing blinders to blatant issues makes them go away – truly a case of eyes wide shut!

It is our hope that we can turn that kind of thinking on its ass – pun intended – and help create a level playing field, equalizing the power between the less fortunate and those who've gained their fame and fortune at their expense.

So brace yourselves, 'cause it's going to be a really fun, fair and fortunate ride!

PART II
SEXUAL EMPOWERMENT

Chapter 8

Sexual "Chemistry" – Working our Wiring

While many a song has been written about the mysteries of love and lust, when it comes down to it, a lot of it is nothing more than a biologically precise dance between the intricate molecules in our brains and our life experiences, driven by our evolutionary imperatives, generating behaviours which can either draw us together or pull us apart. The good news: it makes it that much easier for us to be able to navigate the convoluted maze, not to mention understand why we can fall for the wrong people, cheat on the ones we love, be unable to resist temptation, and so on – a truly empowering feeling.

And as far as sexual power goes, those strong forces make it all the more potent, considering that a combination of erotic desire and the love it leads to is one of the most powerful forces in the world, possibly because romantic passion is one the most powerful circuits in the brain.

Dr. Helen Fisher, author of *Why Him Why Her: Finding Real Love By Understanding Your Personality Type* (28), has done extensive research into the biochemistry behind our personalities and how it plays into who we're drawn to. In her book, she covers all her findings and conclusions rather comprehensively, making it a great attraction bible, with valuable insights into the entire process.

Among other things, her personality tests have identified four personality types, each of which is associated with specific genes within a specific neurotransmitter system. The four types are:

EXPLORERS:
Explorers are curious, creative, adventurous, sexual, impulsive, self-reliant, enthusiastic, spontaneous, optimistic, aggressive, risk takers. They're also novelty/sensation seekers, since they can easily get bored. Their traits are associated with the specific genes in the *dopamine* system. When you meet them, they're most likely to ask you what you *do*. The word they often use is *adventure*. Explorers trust their impulses. And they look for playmates, therefore are drawn to other explorers.

BUILDERS:
Builders are calm, persistent, loyal, traditional, social, cautious, cooperative, managerial, rule-abiding, conscientious, orderly, think-before-you-leap types, who are skilled at building social networks and managing people. Their traits are associated with the genes in the *serotonin* system. They are most interested in what you *know*. The word they use quite often is *family*. Builders trust their values. And they look for helpmates and thus fall for other builders.

DIRECTORS:
Directors are analytical, decisive, focused, direct, inventive, competitive, independent, strategic-minded, tough, exacting, blunt, logical, confident, aggressive, uncompromising, emotionally contained, inflexible, non-tolerant, loners, who are the least compassionate of all types, and can in fact be downright insulting. Their traits are associated with genes in the *testosterone* system. They want to learn about what you *think*. The word they often use is *intelligent*. Directors trust their logic. They look for mind-mates, and match up well with negotiators. But it can get a bit tricky because negotiators look for a

deep and meaningful connection, whereas directors can look for a sexual one, since they have the highest sex drive – and once you whet their sexual appetite, it leads to more sex, via a feedback loop, secondary to an increase in testosterone levels, so they can be hard to keep up with.

NEGOTIATORS:
Negotiators are imaginative, verbal, intuitive, agreeable, introspective, social, emotionally invested/expressive, co-operative, sympathetic, nurturing, idealistic, altruistic, mentally flexible, trusting, sentimental, integrity protecting, connection seekers, who can easily get hurt. They see the big picture and are good at reading people, plus they are the most empathetic of all groups. Their traits are associated with the genes in the *estrogen* system. They like to inquire about how you *feel* about things. The word they use quite often is *passion*. Negotiators trust their intuition. And they look for soul mates and respond especially strongly to directors. Since they're the easiest people to get along with, they often have a lot of suitors.

It's important to note that each personality type is generally drawn to a particular personality type. To learn about your own personality type and that of the person you wish you cast a spell on, it's imperative that you take Dr. Fisher's Personality Tests in her book *Why Him Why Her: Finding Real Love By Understanding Your Personality Type* (28). It'll also teach you what type of language to use with a given individual – something that Neuro-Linguistic Programming also emphasizes (more on that later).

Beyond that, some generic principles that *work* our chemistry to *create* chemistry include:

- Proximity
- Familiarity
- repeated exposure
- unattainability
- voice
- similar values
- ability to have one's needs met
- potential to be loved/adored
- a sense of danger since it stirs up quite the hormonal cocktail

o Looks: perhaps one of the most important factors, since good looks are associated with a plethora of positives; research shows that when we find someone to be attractive, we regard them to be confident, smart, stable, friendly, sensitive, financially secure, generous, healthy, popular and so on – traits that most people look for in a potential mate, creating an enchanting impact. Now while our personality type – and the biochemistry which goes along with it – creates a magnetic pull which draws people together, and the above factors facilitate the generation of initial chemistry, how we communicate is the third part of the attraction trifecta.

In this context, how we communicate refers to our preferred modality – aka our favourite sense that we use to perceive, processes and memorize information, which in turn affects the language style we employ. According to the exact science of Neuro-Linguistic-

Programming (NLP), there are three language styles, based on preferred sensory modalities: visual, auditory, and kinesthetic. Each of us favours one over the others.

Whether you're trying to seduce someone, make them fall for you, or simply mold them to your will, if you know what their primary sensory language is and you're able to speak to it, you'll connect with them in an extremely powerful way. It's the difference between speaking to someone in their first language, versus a foreign language which they don't understand.

As Mark Twain put it, "The difference between the right word and the almost right word is the difference between lightening and the lightening bug." since words are truly electric, especially when it comes to drawing particular people to ourselves.

Visuals need to visualize details and use graphic words to paint them just so. Auditories love talking until they can get a sense of the whole story. Kinesthetics tend to be touchy feely and thrive on sensations, feelings, and movements.

So telling a visual person that they aren't listening to you – when you can both clearly *see* that they're standing right in front of you – will only alienate them; as will painting a graphic picture for an auditory person; or misunderstanding the touchy feely nature of a kinesthetic person.

On the other hand, using the right language will make one feel that they can really talk to you and be understood – i.e. click with you – in the fastest way possible, so you can make a great first impression, which can later be parlayed into a comfortable and lasting connection.

So exactly how do we identify preferred modalities and sensory languages? Using the science of NLP, look for the following clues:

VISUALS (55%)

o obsessed with looks – theirs and other peoples – they are often sharp dressers (which impacts who they attract and are attracted to)
o fast talkers, who often use hand gestures while they talk
o meticulous
o great at remembering faces, not necessarily names
o eyes look up to left when they recall, right when they construct s story (or lie)
o use expressions such as "see what I mean", "I see," "looks good" etc.

AUDITORIES (15%)

o obsessed with talking; often good communicators
o talk with average speed
o dress average
o exceptional at remembering names, facts and details, but not necessarily faces

o eyes move from side to side (between ears) – left when recalling, right when constructing a story (or lying)

o use expressions such as "I hear ya", "in a manner of speaking", "I don't like the tone we're setting" etc.

KINESTHETICS (30%)

- comfort obsessed
- comfy dressers – usually not too concerned with looks
- guys often have facial hair

o   really fit or really slobby, depending upon whether they enjoy the physicality of exercise or the comfort of the couch

- touch and gesture a lot, and often pace – very entertaining to watch
- very touchy feely, so often attract sensitive people
- talk slowly and express details

o   eyes move down to heart when talking – left for recall, right for constructing a story (or lying)

o   use expressions such as "she crawls under my skin", "he rubs me the wrong way", "I feel something's wrong" etc.

Once you know a person's *favourite/ primary* modality, since there can be some blending between all three, you can speak to it and make that connection.

They call it "chemistry" for good reason, since it's about the right biochemical ingredients being mixed together with a sophisticated level of finesse – a skill-set that's worth mastering, if you're to make the most of your sexual power!

Chapter 9
Sexual Know-how

One of my favorite tasks is facilitating sold-out workshops and lectures on the art of seduction and gaining sexual power. I have people from all walks of life, ages, cultural backgrounds, shapes, sizes, professions, orientations and whatnot, jam-packed like sardines, trying to learn the art form. If a fire inspector were to ever come in, we'd get busted for the heat in the room as well as breaking regulation on max room capacity. But seeing the transformations which take place, I'm willing to take that risk!

Once we're all cozied up and giggling with anticipation, we begin by discussing the importance of loving our bodies, self-confidence, knowing what we want, and having the right attitude. It sets the ideal backdrop for everything which follows.

Next, we move into a discussion about creating the right *sense*-ual experience for our prey – generally men in this case – by stimulating their senses the right way, since that's the quintessential ingredient to casting a magical spell.

Our brain processes information in two ways – conscious and sub-conscious. While the former understands language and logic, the latter is too primitive and can only process what it perceives through the five senses, which is why we can intellectually know something, but can't feel it in our heart and soul – those can only be reached through our senses. Once that happens, the messages become a part of our gut instinct and click in in auto-pilot. Small wonder hypnotists engage the senses to change our thought patterns at a visceral level.

It goes to reason then, we can employ those same tools to make our subliminal seduction all the more powerful, so it reaches people's minds, bodies, and souls!

Allow me to share the "sense-ual" part of our workshop.

SMELL:
Smell is the most primal instinct, when it comes to anything sexual. As well, it builds the strongest sense memory. Naturally, that inspires people to use scented candles to create the perfect ambiance. But what that does is, build a sense memory for something other than your own smell. So if you'd rather have your mark get excited the minute he smells you, put your own cologne on light bulbs and let them heat up over time, to create the ultimate sense memory. Spraying the sheets and pillows also works, if you're planning on spending any time there.

Another downside to scented candles is, as they heat up, they start to feel heady and nauseating, making 85% of men lose their erection and the excitement associated with it, by activating the wrong part of the brain.

Beyond that, another way that you may use his nose to create an even more potent effect is, by allowing him to access your natural pheromones. In scrubbing, waxing, deodorizing, we often do away with their powerful impact. So make sure that you use them to your full advantage.

How so? Once you've had a hot and steamy shower – possibly with a bit of ménage a moi – imagine the most sensual experience that you can recall. Your girly parts will start to feel moist in response to it, as you secrete your powerful essence – rich in your pheromones. Dip your finger into your wet juices and then dab some onto your pulse points, just like perfume. You won't need much, and you won't be able to really smell it, but it works its magic nonetheless, without anyone ever realizing it.

But moderation is the key. A lady tried this after attending one of my seminars; when she couldn't smell anything, she decided to take things into her own hands, to generate a more obvious scent. The result was obvious alright, but not in the way she'd intended. Done the right way, you'll have his attention, without him ever knowing what hit him.

When I first heard about it, my girlfriends and I decided to test out the theory. We chose a dance club as our laboratory, where we knew that we could count on the same clusters of men, standing in the same corners, week after week, since consistency was crucial to our experiment. The first time we went, all those in the cluster of men checked us out – as to be expected – from their own comfort zones, but they didn't make any moves.

The following Saturday, we went back there, after dabbing on the "goods," dressed identical to the previous week, right down to the shade of lipstick – this was supposed to be a "scientific, double-blind" study after all, so we couldn't have any additional variables. This time, we couldn't keep them away – they bought us drinks, asked us to dance, and dry-humped us on the dance floor, while we just relaxed and enjoyed our sexual power.

Another story worth sharing involves a woman who took the workshop and started to "get her dab on," whenever she needed to control a situation – talk about power play. It worked rather successfully, every single time.

A couple of years later, she invited me to lead a bachelorette party for her best friend. It was being held in her gorgeous penthouse, overlooking the twinkling city on one side and the sparkling lake on the other, with the most stunning features and furnishings. Blown away, I commented on how her place looked more like a movie set than a regular home – complete with a hot tub, fireplace, palms, and a Moroccan divan on her terrace. She laughed and shared that she paid for it by "getting her dab on."

As a salesperson, she was close to the bottom of her company's corporate ladder, barely making her minimum quota – so much so that she was terrified of getting fired. Seeing that most of her clients were male, she decided to extend her dabbing ritual to her professional life, since she needed to get a control of that situation as well. It worked like a charm – her sexual power allowed her to climb to the very top of that ladder, with millions of commission bucks to boot. She made salesperson of the year two years in a row, without once crossing any professional lines – just the secretive use of her pheromones.

SOUND: While romantic mood music may be Hollywood's idea of the perfect seduction, it can hinder men, by activating the wrong part of the brain. So if you can turn down the music once you start to fool around, and make sure it's vocal-free, you'll keep him from "singing" along in his head, and messing with the mating dance.

Erotic words, on the other hand – picked by 97% of men as the number one aphrodisiac according to a *Men's Health* magazine survey – engage the right part of the brain, in the right way. How else do you think a multi-billion dollar telephone sex industry can survive, at a time when there's so much free porn out there? Without words and sounds, a sensual/sexual experience feels like watching an amazing movie on mute – how exciting is that – even horror flicks can't get a rise out of us if we were to watch then on mute.

The right words also allow us to share our fantasies, and ask for what we want in bed, when someone won't stop and ask for directions. So unless you have a GPS installed in your erogenous zones which can instruct your amour to move a few millimetres in either direction – something that guys can handle, versus you telling them where to go – you'd better master your oral/aural skills. But you have to do it the right way, using your huskiest voice – since it mimics the testosterone-rich, oxygen-deficient voice of arousal.

And what you say is equally important – it's always better to praise what's working and ask for what else you'd like, versus criticizing what isn't working. "A little higher ... not quite ... darn it, you almost had it" will make him feel that you never stop telling him what to do. But a husky "Oh Baby, that feels sooo good ... a little higher and you'll take me right over the edge" will have him feeling like a porn star, thanks to the impact he feels he's having on you, which will make him more than happy to oblige – at the end of the day, men are more invested in our pleasure than we realize, even when it's just to prove their sexual prowess.

To make the experience all the more powerful, take a tip from telephone sex line operators: use the words your target is using, in their tone and volume, engaging their primary sensory modality, to get the biggest bang for your buck.

TOUCH:
When it comes to touch, there are three key points to remember:
o   With the skin being the largest and most accessible sex organ, you can play with it to your max advantage. Any form of stimulation that you can think of – stroking, kissing, nibbling – causes an increase in circulation, which in turn increases sensitivity in the area, making everything feel at least twice as good.
o   Touch along a curvy line is always more delicious than touch along a straight line, since nerve endings expect the pathway of a straight touch, but tingle like mad with the anticipation of a curvy touch, which may or may not make it their way. And of course the increased surface area of the curvy touch also acts as an added bonus.
o   Some nerve endings are touch and pressure sensitive, others are temperature sensitive. Try to excite them all, by playing with mint or ice-cubes to cool the skin down, and blowing warm breath to heat it back up. When we don't play with temperature changes, half of our nerve endings remain uninvolved – why not double the pleasure?

TASTE:
As far as taste goes, anything from diet, to degree of hydration, medication, stress, alcohol consumption, and nicotine – among other things – can have a huge impact. So no matter where the kisses are being

planted, make sure your diet is rich in fresh fruits –
especially pineapple, strawberries and kiwi fruit – and
clear of garlic, onion, strong spices, asparagus,
artichokes, and anything else which smells funky.
FYI, since kissing stimulates all five senses, it's worth
investing in sweet kisses. As well, kisses reduce your
stress hormones and increase your bonding
hormones, convey important genetic information
regarding suitability, and trigger sexual craving, since
men's saliva is rich in testosterone – the reason why
men like wetter kisses than women.

What's more, couples who have a meaningful ten
second kiss before they part ways in the morning, and
another one when they reconnect at the end of the
day, are infinitely closer, with higher levels of oxytocin
– the bonding hormone, aka "the stay versus stray
hormone" as some therapists call it. And it's a lot
more powerful than most people realize – all other
things being equal, their divorce rate is one in ten
versus the North American average of one in two. So
whether you're just getting to know each other, or
have known each other your entire lives, kisses can
definitely seal the deal, making the term "sealed with
a kiss" pretty potent.

SIGHT:
Being visual creatures, men love the right visual
stimuli – from how you're dressed (peekaboo is
always better than letting it all hang out), to the color
you're wearing (red's the sexiest), to your makeup
(lipstick and shadow draw most men, provided they're
not too dark), to what your surrounds look like, to
whatever you do to get their attention. That said, if
you're worried about how you look naked, don't; it's a
big turn-on for men. So leave the lights on; but if

you're self-conscious, throw some red scarves around all the lamps that are turned on, since red light creates a soft focus. Furthermore, red is also the subliminal color for seduction, so why not create a little red light district of your own, and double your benefits?

Once you get to your prey's subconscious, by working all five of his senses, you would've already created a lasting impression. All that's left at this point is, playing with your body language to give off the right cues, since those crawl under one's skin as well, in delicious, subliminal ways – which is crucial, especially when that's your first shot at getting someone's attention, if you weren't fortunate enough to be in charge of a planned seduction in the first place. Here's a rundown on what really works.

Common Seductive Cues Via Body Language

o   Preening: Anything from a hair flip, to running fingers through your hair, to smoothing out your clothes shows interest.

o   Open body language: Exposed neck, open stance (uncrossed arms/legs), and upwards facing palms signal that you're open to meeting someone.

o   Intention cues: If a woman strokes her arm/neck/drink, dangles a shoe from her toe, licks her lips, or tries to get closer to a man, she's signalling her intention to get to know him better.

o   Parading: When a woman walks with an arched back, stomach in, chest out, head high and hips swinging from side to side, she's assuming a "presenting position" – the way that primates signal their desire to mate. Wearing high heels can accomplish all of that in the easiest way possible, along with creating an orgasmic visual, thanks to the pointed toe. Small wonder they've always been a part of the fashion industry – from platforms dating back to the 1600's, to the modern day 6-8 inch lethal dagger stilettos. But walking in them is an art form – one foot in front of the other, leading from the hips, as if you're being pulled by a leash that's attached to your belly button, for max effect. If you can place your hands on your hips, all the better, since it will create the illusion of an hour-glass figure, which gives off a strong fertility signal – men are wired to get turned on by that. FYI, to pull all that off with finesse, pick the heels with the longest sole possible (for max stability), and the highest heel that's right for you – the measure from the tip of your big toe to the end of your heel, divided by two, will give you the right measurement for the highest heel you should aim for, without straining your back.

o   Lordosis: Lordosis is a come-hither pose, universally employed by mammals to give a copulatory invitation. This builds upon the parading posture; in that, the woman walks away from a man, assuming the back arch, butt protrusion, etc., and then looks over her shoulder for a moment to gaze directly into his eyes. It's a way of catching his attention when "in heat", since movement makes people take notice. This is really important for humans – unlike other species, we have concealed ovulation, so we have to put out the right signals to titillate hot pursuit.

o   Copulatory gaze: To show interest, you whether need to look at someone for three or more seconds, look away, and then return your gaze, you're assuming lordosis or not. If that feels like an awkwardly long time, try the "flirting triangle", where your gaze sweeps across one's left eye, right eye, chin, followed by you looking away, then cocking your head to a side and repeating in the other direction, starting with the right eye the second time around.

Smile: If you can give an open mouthed smile, exposing your upper teeth, the other party's mirror cells will make them mimic the same pose, thereby triggering their facial nerves into releasing brain chemicals which make them feel good.

Once you have someone's attention, you need to complete Dr. Perper's mating dance, to seal the deal.

Dr. Perper's Mating Dance:

When we meet someone new who we're attracted to, our hard-wiring starts a basic ritual, involving five simple steps which decide whether we'll make it or break it, as far as future liaisons go.

Dr. Perper, in his extensive research, has identified those steps as follows – if either party brakes the sequence, even accidentally, the couple drifts apart.

1. Eye Contact Via Non-Verbal Signs Which Make One's Presence Known: glance, nod, smile, noticeable movement

2. Verbal Contact: a simple hello, an intro, or a simple ice-breaker (nothing cheesy, witty, or complicated)

3. Turning toward Each Other: first the heads, then the shoulders, and gradually entire bodies must face each other.

4. Slightest Physical Contact: barely noticeable brush or "accidental" touch, reciprocated by a similar touch, followed by eye contact perusing the body oh-so-subtly.

5. Synchronization: This is automatic body language mirroring and voice tone synchronicity – it's in us, just look at babies and the mimicking games they play

FYI, most of us will carry out this ritual in auto-pilot, without even realizing it. Romantic love may thus blossom, provided the "chemistry" is right; but at the very least, the seductive process would've begun.

By now, with an arsenal of knowledge under your belt – embracing the biological, bio-chemical, innate wiring, body language, preferred sensory modality, sense work, and ritualistic behaviors – you should be feeling really empowered.

But none of that matters if you don't have the confidence to use what you've learned – truly imperative to sexual power.

Chapter 10

Sexual Confidence

When it comes to orgasms I'm seriously opposed to the notion "fake it until you make it."

But when it comes to sexual confidence, I feel there's great merit in that mindset, because when we think we're alluring, we ooze the confidence which attracts people; and that in turn allows us to start believing in ourselves.

Sophia Loren knew that principle all too well and she said: "Sex appeal is 50% what you got and 50% what they *think* you got!" meaning, where our natural gifts/abilities end, our confidence can make up for the rest. And over the long haul, it's crucial, regardless of whether or not it's filling any gaps, because our sexiness can only *attract* a suitor, our confidence *sustains* their interest.

Toward that end, I've always believed that sexiness is never about the body we have, it's about the *attitude* we have towards whatever body we got – and how confidently we can project it to the world.

I've known many fashion models who can't hold a candle to ordinary girls when it comes to sexual confidence, because they're critical of themselves, while many girl-next-door types are quite happy with who they are – and know exactly how to work it.

Relationship and sexuality guru, Dr. Marylou Naccarato, has put it another way, that's even more powerful: "I accept my body as imperfect. It gives me breath and gives me life. What matters most is how I carry myself, not how my body carries me."

Embrace those concepts and act as if you love yourself, even when you're not feeling it, and see what happens. Once you experience the magic, and realize that it's still just you, you'll be able to use that power effectively. With time, you'll eventually start to believe in your sexual power.

That said, I'd be lying if I didn't admit that thinking we're alluring doesn't come easily to most, since several of us have spent some time in the self-loathing penalty box.

Isn't it high time that we come out to play, by believing in ourselves enough to have the confidence which fuels sexual power?

Giacomo Casanova was no stranger to that way of thinking. He was an ordinary man who lacked looks, fame or fortune, but he was able to sexually captivate any and every one he laid his eyes on – even women of the cloth and royalty – at a time when sexual liberties weren't easily negotiable. His secret: believing in himself and making the object of his desire his entire focus in the moment, treating each event as if he were "about to propose," and according to him, he was – "something far more delicious than marriage."

Point being, if you believe you're worthy, others will also, since *you're* the one who communicates your self-worth, for better or for worse.

Once you can project how worthwhile you are, if you make them the focus of your attention, they'll be mesmerized by you, and ready to surrender to your wishes – almost as if you've bestowed an honour upon them. But you need to be truly engaged and responsive, to create the kind of magic that leaves people weak in the knees, ready to bow down at your command.

That said, confidence remains an important part of the equation, because focus without confidence doesn't work – it can backfire in fact. We've all had those guys who were really into us but only irritated us because they acted in pathetic ways. And our lack of interest in them made us feel like we were a touch above them, flaming their desire all the more.

So how exactly do you start your journey to gain sexual confidence? By emulating someone who you admire in that arena. For me, it was the character Samantha Jones from the *Sex and the City* television series. She'd walk into a room with her head held high – her tits following suit – and command the attention of everyone within visible distance.

I debuted my Samantha impersonation when I had to a tackle a socially frightening situation. I thought, *I can either walk in and try to be as invisible as the Emperor's New Clothes, or rock my little red dress like Samantha would.* It was a no-brainer. I chose the latter and marched into the room, pretending to be her – way easier than playing myself.

Well, guess what happened: I almost got the same attention that she would – I say "almost" because I allowed myself to shrivel back when the heat became more than what I could handle.

But at the end of day I realized that it was still me, not Samantha, who people had responded to.

Now, many people tell me that they try to emulate *me* – or they want to *be* me, in fact – because they're convinced that I ooze confidence and have the most magical life of all.

While I'm fortunate enough to say that my life feels quite magical indeed, little do they know that despite over a thousand hours in front of a TV camera, I still feel a bit gun shy and anxious at the beginning of every show – that is, until I get wrapped up in my callers' stories.

Regardless, once I reached the point where I was considered to be a veteran, I was asked to create and facilitate a workshop for women, on self-confidence as a way of gaining power, particularly in relationships. I decided to title it "From Doormat to Diva." Read on!

FYI, even though the following principles you're about to read are directed at women, they can be used by anyone – they aren't intended to be either gender specific, or hetero-normative.

Chapter 11

From Doormat to Diva

The word "bitch" generally implies all manner of unpleasant characteristics which should have any man running. Yet, one of the most common questions I get from women is, "Why do men love bitches?" suggesting anything but.

So I decided to survey hundreds of men on this inconsistency, by putting it out there on the radio show I was hosting, since it was "talk radio for guys" after all. Their answers were consistent along the theme that it was the "bitch's" attitude toward *herself* that was attractive, not necessarily her attitude toward them. They respected the fact that she held her own and wouldn't dare treat her in unacceptable ways, since she simply wouldn't put up with it.

Such women are their own gatekeepers – they choose what they will and will not allow to enter their lives – and they can be a lot of fun. It isn't any different from a bad boy's appeal – women always try harder to impress them, because they know they're not enslaved to anyone.

The word bitch in this context is what we touched upon earlier in the book – i.e. **B**abe **I**n **T**otal **C**ontrol of **H**erself. So much so that even when she's dressed to impress, as biographer and novelist Elizabeth Ruth put it, "Her ass is her own, until she needs a good spanking. Even then, she's nobody's slut but the slut inside ...."

Such a woman defines her own ever-changing parameters. She yearns to connect, but will never be compromised or determined by that need; which is not to say that she will never compromise. But when she does, it's truly a compromise, not her becoming lesser for someone else to feel greater.

Furthermore, she will never chase anyone, show jealousy, or let her emotions run the show; for she knows that it will only give someone power over her. If she doesn't like it, she'll deal with it in ways that don't undermine or humiliate her. She realizes that the person with the biggest reaction is the least powerful, so she stays in control.

Her tough-as-nails exterior and assertiveness are valued in men but devalued in women; but to her, anything less is internalized misogyny. Speaking of which, you'll never hear her accuse men of mistreating her, since she simply won't allow it. Besides, how attractive is that?

What's attractive is her attitude, her edge, her disregard for what others think, when she's being true to herself. The only approval she craves is that which comes from within. She believes in herself enough to make others believe in her. Wherever she goes, whatever she does, it's by choice – her choice – as such, she goes through life enjoying herself.

So what's in a word like "bitch"? Attitude, attitude, and more attitude! Let's then look at how you can acquire that attitude, so you'll have everyone swooning at your feet, to worship the Diva within you.

First of all, let's get one thing straight: nice is not an attitude, it's a condition, that generally opens one up to being taken advantage of – quite the opposite of what a Diva is all about.

If you ask ten people to describe a nice girl, nine will talk about what she does for others, with very little value placed on her, without the context of others. And she knows it, judging by the way she too constantly places others above herself – giving, but rarely receiving.

Just to be clear, I'm not talking about humanitarians and the altruistic work they do. I'm talking about those who keep trying harder and harder, all in the hopes of recognition and reciprocity. But trying harder when someone isn't appreciating you to begin with, is as useful as a foreigner speaking louder and louder to someone who doesn't speak their language, hoping to make their point. It just isn't going to happen.

So if you're one of those people who's always planning her life around others, perhaps waiting for an opportunity to let someone else make you happy, wake up. The best that can happen is, you'll get to tag along for something someone else wants to do; the worst, you'll be furious that they didn't grant you that privilege.

Beyond that, here's a list of a few other areas where nice girls could use an attitude adjustment:

o   Nice girls often find themselves chasing after men, but all that guarantees is those men running away; if they chase them in stilettoes, wearing nothing more than a sexy thong, it'll guarantee them getting screwed first.

Divas make their own plans, which may or may not include heels, a sexy thong, or men, for that matter.

o   Nice girls tend to wear their hearts on their sleeves. When they're upset, they talk too much and keep going on and on – often repetitiously – trying to explain themselves, because they've been misunderstood.

Divas never degrade themselves that way – why waste time on someone who can't be bothered to see your point of view in the first place? A Diva only speaks when she knows there's something to be gained. She won't make herself vulnerable otherwise.   To her, information is power – giving it away to someone who may abuse it, is nothing short of insanity.

o   Nice girls generally take on too much upon themselves.

Divas know that if you act like you're capable of doing everything, you'll end up doing everything, so they never have a hard time saying "no", and may in fact use their sexual power to have someone else pick up their own slack.

o   Nice girls don't know how to walk away from a negotiation that isn't working – they keep trying harder and harder until they're either hurt and/or exhausted.

Divas love themselves enough to walk away from a conversation that's going nowhere. She'll break contact until it can be re-established on mutually respectable terms. As John F. Kennedy put it - "Never negotiate out of fear." Her walking away shows she isn't afraid of the consequences.

o   Nice girls give first, negotiate reciprocity later.
Divas don't give until they know it's going to be reciprocal. This ties in really well with forthright negotiations, discussed in Part I of the book.

Is being a Diva starting to sound like a good idea to you? If so, here are the rules she lives by. But not every rule will apply to everyone, or for that matter apply in the same way – a lot will depend upon your relationship status, among other things. But each principle can still apply, to one degree or another.

Divas Hold Their Own

Being a Diva is not about doing away with anyone, particularly not men – in fact, it isn't about men at all. It's about self, self, and more self – as in, self-reliance, self-love, and self-confidence. Men are just a juicy little extra on a Diva's wish list, not her need list. Ironically, men can't wait to do things for her, even though she may present no need.

A Diva knows now to stand up for herself. She won't beg anyone for respect; she'll simply ignore those who won't give it to her. Eleanor Roosevelt once said, "No one can make you feel inferior without your consent."

Diva Won't Compare Herself to Others

Any time a woman is compared to another – whether she does it herself or someone else does it for her – she's demeaned in the process. A Diva knows this. So if her man dares to compare her unfavourably, she will be the first one to send him packing, instead of trying to change herself to please him. Why would she? She's the best. And if he can't see that, she'd rather upgrade her partner than downgrade herself.

Trying too hard is like waving an insecurity flag that sends him racing. Don't kid yourself by saying that you're trying to walk the extra mile; back off a little and let him come to you. And if he doesn't, so what? Don't let fear of losing him run your life. The person who's least fearful and dependent upon the relationship controls the relationship.

Divas Appreciate the Thrill of the Chase

Like it or not, men are hunters: they get up at odd hours, dress up in odd clothes, head out to ungodly odd places, and sit quietly for hours on end, just so they can "hunt" and bring home a goose that a woman could have "gathered" at the supermarket for a tenth of the cost. But the ritual is important to them, since they take pride in being able to chase and catch for themselves.

If you buy a goose and present it to him so you can save him the trouble, you'll ruin his desire. Ditto for when he's chasing after you. So why mess with the chase? And never ever chase him, because the person in the front always ends up being ahead – as do his/her needs. Besides, a guy will either call you psycho for chasing after them – why else would you do something so crazy (geese know better than to chase after men) – or downright ignore you for overdoing it, hoping you'll go away.

Divas refuse to be taken for Granted

Men know which women will act as back-up. They'll first try out for the Diva, and if they come up empty handed, then they'll know exactly who to call – the old-'n-reliables-with-no-pride. Don't let that be you. Never think, *at least he approached me; now all I have to do is show him such a good time that I'll have him hooked and coming back.* The only time he'll come back is when he strikes out again.

So the next time a guy takes you for granted, don't reward him by trying harder, hoping that he'll notice. Walk away! That's it, just go for a walk ... do your own thing ... make your own plans ... and let him be shocked. If you do that, you can be darn sure that he'll take notice. Only *you* can allow him the taking-for-granted privilege, by putting up with it.

Divas are Never Needy

A Diva takes care of her own needs, hence she can be choosy about the men she allows in her life. If she were dependent upon men, her neediness would make her compromise her integrity, and possibly safety. But her independence allows her to choose men for their own sake.

A Diva's financial freedom gives her not only the power to choose how she lives, but also the power to choose how she expects to be treated, and leave when it doesn't feel right. Too many women stay in horrible situations, relying on a dreadful partner, because they aren't financially independent.

A Diva enjoys her own company enough to eliminate that desperate fear of loneliness. If her own hand needs to indulge her once in a while, she sees it as being touched by someone who really loves and respects her.

If she needs to be spoiled by some retail therapy, she knows that the person who pays off her credit card bill will never humiliate her by demanding an explanation. A friend of mine got carried away on her girls' night out and had a little too much to drink. Later, they all went to see a psychic, who sold her a three-thousand dollar amethyst rock, telling her that it would change her energy and chi. Drunk out of her mind, she didn't think much of it and plopped her credit card in front of the crystal ball. Next day, when she woke up, she called me with "good news and bad news". I asked her to tell me the bad news first. She shared, "I bought a fucking three-thousand dollar rock last night – not sure what I was thinking. Good news: I don't have to explain it to a guy, or fight with him, when my head hurts and I'm hung over."

Bad decisions aside, ironically, a Diva's self-sufficiency makes men crave her all the more and want to do things for her. They want to capture her and create a need, lest she slip away. They are terrified of losing her, since they know that instead of waiting in the wings for him, she always has men waiting for her.

Not being needy will liberate both yourself and your relationship. Remember you did just fine before you met him, and will again, with or without him. *He* needs to need *you*, for him to stay! He may be attracted to your looks at first, but it's your sexual power and likeability that'll make him wanna stay and please you!

Divas Never Take Things Personally

A Diva knows better than to take anything negative personally. She's a legend in her own mind and she'll be damned if she doesn't make herself a legend in everybody else's minds as well. Someone who can't handle that is probably too weak to be with her in the first place. Know that 90% of put downs and rejections have nothing to do with you. External circumstances and internal insecurities cause people to lash out and/or reject.

Love the Diva within you enough to never believe anything that isn't consistent with all the good stuff you know about yourself. And become the girl who feels she deserves the best, be it something she wants, or how she's being treated, and sit back and watch the power of the confidence that emanates from that.

Diva Won't Set Up For Disappointment

A Diva will never have false expectations that can neither be understood nor fulfilled – it keeps her disappointment to a minimum. This doesn't mean that she doesn't have expectations; it only means that she ensures that her expectations are reasonable, and she's comfortable walking away from what is intolerable.

Beyond that, a Diva never goes looking for trouble. If something's not right, she looks for the simplest explanation and doesn't get bent out of shape over it. Simple explanations lead to simple solutions. Over-analysis – aka analysis paralysis – is the greatest source of worry for naught. A Diva knows that, and therefore doesn't waste her time on setting herself up.

Divas Know How to Have a Good Time

Divas know how to have a good time, without becoming a good-time girl. They'll pique one's interest just enough to seal the deal, without giving anything away for no reason. That said, a Diva's own pleasure is always a good enough reason for giving it away. Divas love sex, and can pursue it for its own sake, or as a means to a great end. As such, if a man's a keeper, she'll eat his cock and have it too. But she doesn't need men to have a good time. Men are just lucky to be included, if and when she decides – of course they find that to be irresistible. They want what she's got. Whether they can access it or not, they're going to die trying.

Divas Don't Let Guilt Run their Lives

Divas may feel guilt for not feeling guilty, but that's where it stops. Since they don't hold anyone responsible for their own mistakes, they don't expect to be held responsible for other people's mistakes. If something is going to make her feel bad, she simply won't go for it. But when she goes for something, even if it doesn't work out, it's not a mistake, it's a lesson learned – and when was the last time you felt bad about learning a lesson? It's all in her perspective – which views guilt as a wasted emotion. We all know what's right or wrong – we don't need guilt to nudge us. All guilt can do is stop us from living life fully and happily. As such, when it comes to inconsequential stuff, a Diva would rather say sorry after the fact, versus ask for permission upfront, risking refusal.

Divas Don't Feel a Need to Justify things

While men are goal oriented, women are process oriented. This is why they feel the need to justify everything from why they feel a certain way, to why they bought something, to why they need something. A man will never say, "Honey, I'm feeling a little insecure and would like to know that I still mean the world to you", or "Honey, I know I have ten shirts in my closet but I had to buy this one because I'm feeling fat lately and nothing fits good enough for my presentation next week" or "Honey, I would really appreciate it if you could do such and such for me, since I simply can't", He's more like, "Sorry I barked at ya – really stressed out lately", or "That shirt – yeah!", or "Can you pick up the dry-cleaning on your way home from something" – never mind that something is at the other end of town.

A Diva knows that to relate to a man in his world, she's better off saying, "Oh those stilettoes!" for her hundredth pair, and then move on. She knows that the best person to guard her interests is she herself.

Divas Aren't Thrown Off by Criticism

A Diva's definition of criticism is a difference of opinion on a very important topic – herself. If people can argue passionately about religion, politics, money, and children, of course they're going to have differences of opinion over something equally important – her. There are no right or wrong answers, just opinions. And her opinion of herself is all that matters to her, along with those who agree with her.

If someone doesn't see things her way, she'll listen to what they say, pick what helps her do better, and then not be bothered with the rest. No one can make her feel bad – she simply won't let them. Besides, she knows that it's impossible to be liked by everyone all the time. Ironically, she's liked by most. Men want her, women want to be her!

I used to fall apart when faced with criticism. Now I try to tell myself, well that's just that one person's opinion, and immediately call or e-mail someone who has a better opinion of me, and is willing to stroke my ego to awaken the Goddess within – or at the very least, unleash her power.

Divas Plan Via *Their* Moods Not Others

Being people focussed, it's a female tendency to get bent out of shape if someone else is in a bad mood. They think that it has something to do with them, even though they haven't done anything wrong. Regardless, they take responsibility and try to do what they can to lift the other party's spirits, and possibly feel they're inadequate otherwise.

Divas tell themselves, "I know he/she is in a foul mood, but since I didn't put him/her there, it's not my responsibility to fix it; so I'm going to let him/her wallow until they're ready to come around." Hard as it is, they resist the temptation to intrude and simply walk away, once they've offered to help.

Eventually, the person comes around after fixing their own bad mood, without having to fix any bad blood between them. Bottom line, it's someone else's bad mood, don't make it yours.

Diva's Love Trying on Shoes

Beyond the orgasmic joy of retail therapy –
aka finding the perfect pair of shoes to lift your
spirits in a perfect way – Divas do try on others'
shoes for size from time to time. It allows them
to see things from others' perspectives, thereby
knowing where the other party might coming
from. Can't get any more powerful than that,
because most misunderstandings are based in
perspective, not reality – having the right one
dissipates them.

Divas Invented Mantra: "I'm Worth It"

When I was a little girl, my mother overdid
the humility bit; so much so that I became an
emotional cripple with no self-confidence, very
early on. Relationship after relationship, I was
my own worst enemy, thanks to my lack of self-
esteem – I tolerated abusive situations because I
didn't think I could do better. And I must've
confused humility with humiliation, judging by
how often I put with it.

Divas know that low self-esteem is a
debilitating condition and refuse to give into it.
Like an addiction, it gets worse with time, even
though we know its harmful effects. Why
indulge? Better to indulge in things which make
you feel good, because you're worth it! And if
you're struggling with the humility issue, know
that humility is "thinking of yourself less, not
thinking less of yourself!"

Divas Get: Being Happy Beats Being Right

Ever see one of those car crashes at a stop sign where someone insisted on going through, since they had the "right" of way? Right or not – with or without the support of insurance – they may have made their point, but at what cost? Besides, instead of saving three seconds they'll spend three days getting estimates, not to mention possibly get stuck with a loaner for another thirty days. They may be right, but are they happy?

Most discussions heat up whenever someone tries to prove their point. If in doing so, an argument ensues; what difference does it make who's right at that point?   Besides, your "opponent" will never see you as right in any case, certainly not when their emotions are running the show. Divas know that being happy outweighs being right, so they don't sweat the small stuff at a cost to their happiness. They know how to pick their battles.

Divas Know True Power

If you stroke a man's ego at least as diligently as you stroke his libido, he doesn't need to act tough around you. People only act that way, or get defensive, when they need to defend something – like their pride, for instance. Twisted as it sounds, defensiveness is a fight to impress. Whoever said "A slave is a master in disguise" knew where true power rests – in the hands of the individual who knows how to get the result they want, without being obnoxious, or having to make a point. Those who make a big deal out of small stuff are penny wise pound foolish.

Real power doesn't need to be validated, it just is. Like a rich person with obvious wealth, or someone with obvious beauty, it needs no proof. Real Divas know that when they ask gently and get the right results, they hold the real power – it's about the control you have over yourself, in generating the results you want for yourself. Sherry Argov, author of *Why Men Love Bitches* (29), says, "If you want to enjoy life with real power, agree with everything, explain nothing, and then do what feels best." Divas take that principle to heart, since they needn't prove anything to anyone but themselves. Wish I had that book when I was trying to come up with my own road map.

Bottom line, exercise your power, so you're truly in control of your life, versus allowing someone else to control you. And if you get that feeling like you're losing yourself, follow your feelings to the source and see what they're trying to tell you. Perhaps a childhood wound has been ripped open and it's taken you back to a place where you had no control. That being the case, commit to dealing with those issues. But in the meantime, imagine a stop sign so your brain puts on the breaks and reboots. Then start to look at the situation afresh, and create a shift which honors you, so you can reattempt your magic, from a place of empowerment.

Divas Love Themselves to Bits

A Diva's mantra is not "Love thy neighbour as thyself", it's "Love thyself intensely and your neighbour will be happier living next to you." Either way, Divas end up being happy, and everyone ends up loving them all the more, because they don't feel responsible for their happiness. Divas know that assuming the responsibility for your own happiness ensures that no one else has any control over you.

Divas Don't Nag

Divas believe that one should never claim as a right what can be asked nicely as a favour. But the key is to ask, instead of expecting someone to somehow read your mind – or figure it out in another way – and then nagging them if they don't. Once she's asked nicely, if something still isn't done, a Diva will ask someone else – she never has a shortage of individuals wanting to please her. When her guy sees that other guys are trying to hone in on his territory, he'll more than likely jump to honour her request, to redeem himself in her eyes. Either way, she gets the job done, while using her power versus losing it.

Divas Think Before they Speak

Divas know that men use half the words as women, to parlay minimum details, when absolutely necessary, while their minimum attention span is still intact. A Diva will therefore communicate with him only on a need-to-know basis. She sacrifices quantity for quality – aka enhancing her best interests – saving the former for the gender that appreciates *rapport* talk versus *report* talk. This is why in as much as she might want him for her best friend, she'll look for a friend elsewhere if there's any danger of compromising the lover part. Bottom line, a Diva knows that with a man, less is more – and anything beyond the minimum is a waste. So she exercises impulse control, which is more flattering than the control her Wonder-Bra provides – since it lifts and separates her from the rest.

Divas: Unpredictable, In And Out of Bed

A man can never take a Diva for granted, because he never knows what her next move is going to be. She is feisty, independent, unpredictable, fun, and doesn't bend to his ways, unless bending his way brings her pleasure. That said, she can control her groin, even when he might be controlled by his, and lets him know what needs to happen before it happens – in a sexy voice of course – now that's sexual power! And just as he starts to get the drift, she may exercise her privilege to change her mind yet again, if it pleases her. Never a dull moment with her – keeps boredom at bay.

So if you want to feel powerful like a Diva, follow her rules. Get back in the driver's seat and learn to "drive" your own life. "No" is not a bad word – it can be the most liberating word, in fact.

The easiest place to start is with small, attainable goals, such as, "I promise myself to say no to at least one thing I don't want to do this week, and replace it with a yes to something I'd rather do."

And the next time someone takes you for granted, tell yourself, "There's wasted effort that I won't repeat, and use the time to do something for myself that I've been putting off."

In general, if there's something you want to do/buy for yourself, consider yourself worthy and find the budget to do it. If you don't love and spoil the Diva within you at least as diligently as you would your partner or child, then you're telling yourself and the world that you're inferior to them. I'm not suggesting you become selfish; just take care of yourself *as well* as you do for others. At times, this may mean putting yourself first – that being the case, just remember what they say when you board a plane: "Secure your own oxygen mask before helping anyone else, including your kids" and go forth without guilt or regret.

The power to change your life is in your hands, as is the power to have others please you. And sexual power can be a major engine which drives things for you along those lines, provided you use it fairly and responsibly.

Chapter 12

Giving Ourselves the Permission to Wield Our Sexual Power

As a psychotherapist, I have an inside track on people's struggles. Regardless of what we're looking at, a lot of them revolve around the same issue – i.e. a conflict around an opinion that's being pushed as the *only* right way of doing something, having been established by someone else (generally society) as the normative standard – where all aberrations are deemed reprehensible.

Such forces try to frame our reality, and possibly constrict it, by directing our values and choices in one direction – so much so that we can start to feel like we're fraudulent, living someone else's life.

If those philosophies were *truly* to be the *only* right way, they wouldn't vary from generation to generation – or culture to culture, for that matter.

Take marriage for instance. Stephanie Coontz, author of *Marriage, A History: How Love Conquered Marriage* (30), shares the following historical views on it:

> *"Through most of human history, love was not at all the point of marriage. Marriage was about getting families together, which was why there were so many controls. The notion that a couple*

would marry for love was considered almost anti-social, even subversive; parents could disown their kids for doing it.

... The Greeks thought lovesickness was a type of insanity, a view that was adopted by medieval commentators in Europe.

... In the Middle Ages, the French defined love as a 'derangement of the mind' that could be cured by sexual intercourse, either with the loved one or with a different partner.

... Too much love was thought to be a real threat to the institution of marriage. Earlier proponents of marriage were as horrified by the idea of a love match as late 20th-century people were by [the] idea of same-sex marriage."

Another piece of literature, Richard Zacks' book, *History Laid Bare: Love, Sex, and Perversity from the Ancient Etruscans to Warren G. Harding* (31), addresses the same concepts, in a passage titled "Love between Husband and Wife? Are you Mad?"

"For what is love but the inordinate desire to receive passionately a furtive and hidden embrace? But what embrace between husband and wife can be furtive, I ask you, since they may be said to belong to each other and may satisfy

each other's desires without fear that anybody will object?

... But there is another reason why husband and wife cannot love each other, and that is the very substance of love, without which love cannot exist: jealousy. A married couple should avoid it like the plague, while lovers should always welcome it as the mother and nurse of love."

Later on, the passage groups love, sex, and gluttony together, as sins of the flesh.

"A clergyman ought not to devote himself to the works of love but be bound to renounce absolutely all the delights of the flesh. But since hardly anyone lives without carnal sin, and since the life of the clergy is, because of the continual idleness and the great abundance of food, naturally more liable to temptations of the body than that of any other men."

Now fast forward to present day of the nuclear family, where love and sex are viewed quite differently, and in fact protected by the traditional institution of marriage.

But as Dr. Buss' research revealed – referred to in Part I of the book – sex isn't necessarily tied into love and romance; so if one is to take that narrow view of sexuality, they could indeed become disappointed.

Sex Therapist, Dr. Marty Klein, author of *Sexual Intelligence: What we Really Want from Sex – and How to Get It* (32), has written an article titled, "When Sex Isn't About Sex: Everything in the world is about sex, except sex, which is about power." In it, he addresses the current confusion around the concept of sex being reserved just for love, affection and connection.

Dr. Klein says:

"Sex is sometimes about power. But sex can [also] be about many different things. For some people it means 'I can still get sex,' or 'I can still get sex from a good-looking man/woman,' or 'I can still get sex from you.'... A few more reasons that people want sex [include], to get attention, to get touching, to feel taken care of, to feel attractive, to challenge taboos, to assert autonomy.

... So why does this matter? It matters because if what you want is touching, or attention, or validation, there are many other, usually more effective ways to get them than sex.

... So to help make sex more enjoyable, don't turn it into your all-purpose go-to for every emotional situation. Find other ways in addition to sex to connect, to express yourself, and to feel validated, so sex can be simpler and easier."

It goes to reason then, sex is no more limited to those functions as those functions are limited to sex, as the primary source of fulfilment.

Either way, instead of ignoring history and shaming those who follow their biological instincts, we need to give ourselves the permission to be okay with sex and the power associated with it, in different contexts, provided we're clear on our parameters, because the shame that's associated with thinking outside the box was once seen as sanity – aka the *only* right way at the time.

Furthermore, such forthrightness will free sexual games – and the level playing field where they are played – from being perceived as a manipulative tactic, since fair play is anything but.

It's Mother Nature's way of creating an equalizing force that's greater than any subversive forces, which came into play with the dawn of the agricultural era, and have stayed within the so-called egalitarian era.

So give yourself the permission to master the craft and then own what you do with it.

It makes infinite sense, as far as sexual economics go. Think back on the Diva – can you really argue with her way?

Chapter 13

Wielding our Sexual Power

We talked about the tools of the trade and the art-form, followed by giving yourself the permission to use your sexual power. Now all you have to do is kick-start your new way of life.

Once you begin to see the results, you'll become masters at creating the kind of erotic tension which releases more energy than a biological orgasm, making mind-fucking a lot more satisfying, not to mention the safest form of sex. Remember, sexual power is not about having sex to get what you want – no one needs an instruction manual for that – it's about tapping into primal instincts in delicious and captivating ways, and saving sex for when you feel like it, for whatever reason.

Think of it this way: would you go see a movie with a linear plot? Personally, I love the twists, turns, mystery, sexual tension, drama, etc. driven by the *possibility* of something happening. Once it reaches that climax so to speak, the plot is pretty much over, which is why most series keep the protagonists from sleeping together for as long as they possibly can.

That said, regardless of how you intend to use your sexual power, to keep it fun and fair, you need to wield it for your own sake, on your own terms, respecting some basic guidelines, to get the best results.

Toward that end, let's look at my "**Ten Commandments for Wielding Sexual Power**":

1. *Thou shalt maintain control at all times – remember, patience is a virtue*.

The number one thing which makes people lose their power or become undone is losing control. When you fail to exert self-control, your limbic system flares into action and makes you act out of character, because immediate rewards trump cortex driven restraints.

A classic example of this principle is the famous "Marshmallow Test" conducted by Stanford University in the late 1960s. Basically, four year olds were left with marshmallows while their teacher left the room. They were instructed that they could eat them if they wanted; but if they could hold out until their teacher came back, they'd double their treats. Surprisingly enough, some of the kids were able to wait up to 15 minutes – talk about juvenile abstention! And the benefits of their ability for self-restraint didn't just end there. Long-term follow-up studies showed that a child's capability to delay rewards correlates with academic success, high adult income, and the ability to tolerate stress and rejection – two things, which will come in very handy if you're practicing your sexual power.

2. *Thou shalt do whatever it takes to feel good about yourself, and commit to nurturing it for a lifetime*.

Since we aren't born with self-esteem issues, it's critical to find out when they started and where they came from. I'm a big fan of investing in some therapy to work through unresolved childhood stuff – from lack of parental attention/attunement to actual trauma – so you don't carry that baggage with you throughout your life, or for that matter reincarnate it in all your future relationships. The relationship you have with yourself is the most important one, since it determines all others.

If you are connected to yourself, you never have to feel like you're only a half of a fractured relationship. You can give to yourself, and meet your own needs like you would give to a lover to meet their needs. And if someone amazing comes along to love you the right way, then that's your bonus for working hard on loving yourself – you can cherish them with all your heart and soul at that point.

When you finish taking care of your baggage and start to love yourself the way you were meant to be loved, ignite your passion – enroll in a course or a dance class, hit the gym, and do whatever else makes you feel good.

Once you get there, commit to nurturing and protecting your self-esteem at all costs. Never cheapen yourself by selling out or compromising your core values. It will decrease – not increase – your worth in both your own as well as others' eyes. In other words, know your bottom line and what something will cost you, especially over the long haul, so you never tarnish your self-respect.

3. *Thou shalt not judge anyone – including yourself – particularly around physicality or sexuality*.

Sexiness is a mind-set, not a body look; ditto for what we do with it, depending upon whether or not we're comfortable in our own skin. Furthermore, both of those traits also lie on a spectrum which varies from one person to the next. So how can anyone possibly judge either one – and why should they? Sophia Rinaldis (33), in an article for *Mind Body Green*, on body-shaming behaviours, covers both those points rather well. She says:

a. *Stop judging expressions of sexuality*.

Sexuality can be expressed in the way we choose to reveal our bodies, through clothing or movement. Judging people on the way they do this, or denying certain people the right to express their sexuality based on their body type is a form of body-shaming. Expressing sexuality is a natural human need to which we are all entitled. We should be able to express our sexual identities in the ways that are most genuine to us without being judged for it.

b. Stop defining beauty as a look rather than a state of mind.

When we realize that we're more than just our bodies, we can begin to let go of some of the pressures we place on them. The body is a strong vehicle, but it is not the sole medium through which we experience life. Beauty also comes from attributes such as humor, compassion, selflessness, intelligence.

4. Thou shalt make a conscious effort to learn whatever you can about your mark, come up with a game plan, and then follow through.

This includes vetting, finding out his/her likes, dislikes, interests, and values, discerning his/her primary sensory modality and personality type, and so on. If you don't know your mark, how will you mesmerize them in magnificent ways?

Once you have that information, come up with a game plan – utilizing the tools we've discussed – that's custom-designed to capture your target, and then go for it. But never ever compromise your bottom line – know it ahead of time and what it could cost you if you don't protect it.

5. ***Thou shalt neither push nor rush anything.***

To best illustrate this point, allow me to share an old tale with you:

> *The sun and the wind were really bored one day. Said the wind to the sun, "Let's have a contest." The sun agreed and asked what they'd be competing over. The wind responded, "You see that man walking on that winding road? Whichever one of us can take his jacket off the fastest wins." The sun smiled and agreed, offering the wind a first go at it. The wind huffed and puffed, convinced of its mighty force, but the man only tightened the coat around himself and eventually buttoned it up the whole way. The sun looked rather amused. So the wind challenged it to see if he could do better. The sun shone brightly, making the man really warm. One by one his buttons opened up until they were all undone. Eventually he ended up taking his coat off his shoulders.*

Moral of the story: if you're to use your power, do it gently, so the other party thinks it's their idea; if you're forceful, you'll have a harder time convincing people to surrender to your will. We all want to buy, we just don't want to be sold.

So don't rush into anything, just take it nice and slow, savoring every moment. Let them work for the privilege of being in your universe – even as they do things for you – because the harder one works at acquiring something or someone, the greater value they place on it/them, since it marks a culmination of yearning, not to mention helps justify their efforts. Besides, you'd be messing with the chase if your target is a male.

6. *Thou shalt know when to walk away, with your pride in-tact, without any unpleasant thoughts*.

If after your best efforts it doesn't look like you're likely to win, simply walk away. Fighting with reality never works, and it invariably makes us upset. Byron Katie, author of *Loving What Is: Four Questions that can Change Your Life* (34), asks us to do "The Work" when we start to have doubts or negative thoughts during such moments.

The Work is a simple, straightforward antidote to the unnecessary suffering we create for ourselves. It's not about escaping reality; in fact, it's about embracing it, so you don't torture yourself with resistance.

So what exactly does it entail? It requires you to ask yourself the following four questions, and answer them with all sincerity and utmost honesty.

    a.   Is what I'm thinking / what I believe really true?

    b. Do I know it to be absolutely true – i.e. is it an indisputable fact, or just my impression, inference, or opinion? The only thing that's true without a doubt is what's actually happening – or has already happened – not your interpretation of it.

    c.   How do I react when I think / believe that thought?

    d. Who would I be without that thought – i.e. how would my feelings and life change?

Once you complete that analysis, you'll be able to see the benefit of dropping your negative thoughts, which are especially strong when your demands aren't being met. So embrace the Diva within you and do what she would do under the circumstances, instead of embarrassing yourself.

7. *Thou shalt remember your manners.*

Saying please and thank you, saying sorry, and expressing sincere praise and gratitude are not bad things – give credit where it's due, even as you celebrate your victory, which you must. Narcissists have a hard time saying those things, since they *expect* others to acquiesce to their wants, needs, and whims. Furthermore, they don't like being wrong, nor do they want to feel indebted.

When you respect others, they'll respect you. And win or lose, you can't let your sportsmanship lapse. Think of what would happen if you want those people to be a part of your world in the future?

8. Thou shalt share the sea of possibilities and the wealth of your knowledge with the sisterhood.

There are enough resources and fun to be enjoyed by all. In part I we discussed how a woman with sexual power is generous – people give her things and she loves sharing them with others. Beyond that, she loves sharing her knowhow with other women, since she wants to elevate the entire sisterhood to a great place, versus letting her insecurities run the show, leaving behind the weak and those who don't have her strength and power.

9. Thou shalt remain focused and never get lazy in your pursuit of delightful treasures and seductive power.

It'll lose its deliciousness and potency otherwise. A woman with sexual power is insatiable – she never stops improving herself, since she wants her life to always be increasingly magical. She enjoys the journey so much that she lets it take her wherever there's adventure, because there is no destination which will make her quit; she'll just find another one. She gains experience as she ages – the lines on her face prove it. She delights in what she has – she's not afraid of stretch marks which show that she brought a child into this world; she knows that many women would trade places with her in a heartbeat, just to have the privilege of becoming a mother. Her attitude determines her, not her body. She has a perpetual hunger for knowledge and self-betterment. When she puts her expected landmarks to rest, she begins to live life to the fullest, as a sexually seasoned woman. She's proud of who she is, in every way imaginable, and always believes that *the best is yet to come*.

10.   *Thou shalt use thine sexual power in healthy ways.*

Never use your power to manipulate. Be forthright and take pride in your power versus hiding it like a dirty little secret. Then and only then will you allow it to emerge fully, so you can wield it in a way that will trump fame and fortune.

The experience of obtaining sexual power in this way will leave you feeling inebriated by your new-found passion, and high on the sweet taste of victory. I'm getting a lady wood just thinking about it!

To ensure that nothing takes away from your magnificent experiences, it's important to ensure that you progress with safety.

Chapter 14

Avoiding Sexual Misunderstandings

Jessica Rabbit, Roger Rabbit's human "Toon Wife" in *Who Framed Roger Rabbit*, is one of the most famous sex symbols on the animated screen – her character inspired by actresses like Veronica Lake, Rita Hayworth, and Lauren Bacall. In one sequence, she says to Eddie Valiant, "I'm not bad, I'm just drawn that way," which has become a popular quote – implying that she isn't the salacious character that's inferred by her appearance.

And such is the case with many innocent teen girls who end up looking sexy and sexual when they dress to emulate pop culture, even though they're neither feeling that, nor trying to send any such signals.

It goes to reason then, we have a responsibility to teach the young and the impressionable about how they're coming across – i.e., the power of their sexuality – so they aren't misunderstood, victimized, or traumatized. There's enough sexual trauma in this world as is, that has nothing to do with how one dresses. It'll keep them safe, not to mention make it easier for them to use their sexual power appropriately, when they're ready and able, without reservation or regret.

Sadly, a lot of the older members of the sisterhood treat those young women with disdain, assuming that they're actively trying to lure men –

how is that any different from the men who view them that way? When someone acts out of jealousy in that way, they become both the hurricane as well as the house it destroys.

Isn't it better for us to work together to nurture our youth, so they can enjoy both their innocence as well as their sexual power – when the time comes – in age-appropriate ways?

Such education will also go a long way toward stopping the behaviours which can destroy them, because they don't understand the long-term implications of their actions – sexting, cyberstalking, participation in rainbow parties, *Girls gone Wild* behaviours, and other ill-conceived efforts at securing their fifteen seconds of fame.

Another point of criminal misunderstanding is sexual assault. I for one prefer to call it just assault, without the adjective, since it has nothing to do with sex.

Toward that end, I managed to make my point to a large university audience, decades ago, during a debate where a panel was arguing just that notion.

As I tried to build a case for dropping the word "sexual" from sexual assault, another panelist – a gentleman by the name of Wayne – kept interrupting me, since he felt that it was most definitely a sexual act that just got a little out of hand, seeing that it involved sexual organs.

Irritated, I walked over to Wayne and stroked his left cheek lovingly with my right hand. He nuzzled into my hand like a puppy yearning petting. I asked, "Do you like that?" Wayne nodded a strong affirmative like a puppy now drooling for a bone. To which I responded, "There will be lots more of that if you stop interrupting and let me finish delivering my points."

Once I finished presenting my arguments, I walked over to Wayne – this time *I* was salivating – and struck him on the same cheek with the same hand, and asked, "How did it feel this time? Still pleasurable and affectionate right, 'because it involves the same body parts as previously?'"

Never before, or since, have I struck anyone, or raised a finger to my kids for that matter.

I was fully prepared to be charged with assault, unsure whether Wayne would class it as sexual or not – sorry, I digress. But Wayne was gracious enough to acknowledge the point I was trying to make, and left it at that, while the rest of the audience cheered beyond anything that I could've ever imagined.

Later, many of the women in the audience shared with me, how that way of thinking liberated them from sexual hang-ups they'd carried for ions, tied into their own traumas, because of inappropriate nomenclature. I know the feeling all too well, having experienced it first-hand – the very reason for my passion to do something about it.

A less distressful situation where one can also lose their sexual power is, "friends with benefits" arrangements.

They start off with the understanding that there will never be any romantic involvement of any sorts, just a convenient sexual arrangement with a friend, when either party feels the urge but doesn't have a partner – the idea is to be with someone safe and comfortable, versus cruising for a potentially dangerous one-night-stand. I know many women who find the arrangement to be especially appealing, for those very reasons.

But what most people don't realize is the "law of six" – i.e., mammals either bond or want to distance themselves from their mate, after having sex with them six times, marking the end of a "trial period."

That said, men can continue with a friends with privileges arrangement even when bonding doesn't take place, since it wasn't supposed to be a romantic relationship in the first place; but most women end up wanting to be true to whatever comes up – distancing or bonding.

And if they find themselves in the bonding zone – which is often the case, due to their wiring – they'll try their best to nail a relationship that resides well outside the initial understanding, which can create a power shift if their partner remains in that initial casual zone.

Sexual misunderstandings can also arise with the use of the birth control pill.

When the pill was first made available, women finally had the opportunity to control their sexuality and enjoy it strictly for pleasure, versus procreation.

But what they didn't realize was that being on "the pill" often causes a loss of libido, thereby hindering the very thing they wanted to enjoy.

Furthermore, the pill can lead to women feeling a kinship toward their partner, versus a ravenous sexual hunger, since their body acts as if they're already pregnant, thanks to the hormonal cocktail that's used by the pill to trick the body into thinking just that.

So while the power of the pill may have started off giving women sexual power, we now know that it can often have the opposite impact.

The pill can also hinder a woman's raw sexuality by robbing her of the super power, which emerges during ovulation – and stops when she's taking the pill.

Studies show that women give off certain fertility cues during ovulation – a change in the tenor of their voice, for one – making them more desirable than ever, not to mention feeling super horny. Small wonder exotic dancers make 35% more in tips during ovulation.

But even outside of that special tenor, voice plays a potent role in conveying sexual cues. As previously mentioned, when a woman is aroused, her voice starts to sound husky.

So if you can master that tone even otherwise, you'll be able to convey desire and thereby desirability, putting a magic spell on the appropriate gender within earshot – the very reason telephone sex operators can get consumers to part with three to five bucks a minute, to have someone speak to them in that tone, repeating back their desires to them.

On the flipside, a high-pitched voice can indicate that whipped feeling, when you're trying to impress someone but your anxiety gets the better of you. It can also indicate a petite stature – height – which is generally considered more attractive by men.

But if you're trying to convey sexy, you're better off with sticking to those husky tones.

When I was asked to host a live, call-in show on "Talk Radio for Guys", the station manager was ecstatic that I could discuss important sexual matters with guys, with a boudoir voice no less, "drenched with throaty, orgasmic undertones".

He joked, "With that voice and knowledge, I'll make you the next Xaviera Hollander".

I never came close to her level of sexual power, fame, or fortune, but I did get recognized by my voice at least as often as my face – from fast food drive-thrus to other moments where my face wasn't clearly visible.

With time, I was asked to do a workshop on talking dirty, deliciously combining tone, content, and desire – a workshop that sells out effortlessly to this day, with erotic talk being the number one aphrodisiac for men.

Moral of the story: if you can understand how sexual power works, you can use it to your advantage, instead of having it work against you, via painful misunderstandings, especially those in your intimate relationships.

The idea is to keep it safe, fun and healthy!

Chapter 15

Keeping it Safe and Healthy

With every new way of life come new responsibilities and challenges. Having sexual freedom and enjoying the power which comes along with it is no different. So keep the following points in mind:

1. ***Just because you can, doesn't mean that you have to.***

Professor Jonathan Zimmerman (35) in his article for Newsworks, on "Sexual Assault in the Hook-Up Era" covers this point rather well:

> *"We've entered a new sexual landscape, which allows our female students much more independence than their predecessors had. That brings a fresh set of challenges that didn't exist in earlier eras, when only so-called "bad girls" had sex ... [who] had to walk a delicate tightrope: keeping chaste could alienate your date, but having sex might harm your "reputation" — and your marital possibilities.*
>
> *... Today, women have much greater freedom to define and experience their sexuality. As a college professor and the father of*

126

two female undergraduates, I'm grateful for that.

... But they face new dilemmas, too. We've gone from a time when only bad girls did it to one where everyone does it, or is expected to. Actually, 40 percent of female college seniors report that they are virgins or have only had intercourse once. But students now feel a new pressure to have sex, and lots of it."

Point being, it is our hope that this book liberates you, versus adding new pressures to be a certain way – so definitely not meant for the naïve or the light of heart.

2. *Never promise what you don't intend to deliver*.

It's one thing to have saucy conversations and pique one's interest in you, or to flirt to add excitement to their life, or be playful in enticing ways, or work "the tools" to cast a spell; but it's quite another to lead someone into believing that you're *promising* sex when you have no intention of keeping your promise. The term "cock-tease" comes to mind in that case – don't you agree? As such, try to stay away from mixed messages, if you don't want to get a nasty reputation.

3. *Know your limits*.

Due to sexual harassment laws, be careful with your sexual power plays in your workplace. As well, if you get as much as a hint the person you're with might not take no for an answer, get out of the situation right away – a man's physical power will trump a woman's sexual power most of the time, if it ever comes to that.

4. *Never make yourself vulnerable in the digital / social media world.*

The minute you send a sext, a salacious email, post anything on social media, or send a picture of yourself to someone, it's available to the whole world. People forward those things all the time – sometimes just to show off. And if you piss someone off then all that's keeping them from humiliating you is just one click.

I've had too many women come to me in tears, wishing they hadn't sent something that's so easily transferrable – reputations are ruined, jobs are lost, marriages are broken up, and children are humiliated. It isn't worth it, even if you think the extra attention or 15 seconds of fame can justify the price.

Think "The Swifter-gate Ordeal": A tween sent a video clip of herself sucking on a *Swifter* mop to a guy she was crushing on. He forwarded it to everyone to show off. At first she loved the male attention. But after her 15 seconds of fame had come and gone, the stigma regrettably remained – there was nothing that she could do at that point to reverse her bad decision. It's very easy to do something – particularly in the diggie world, but impossible to undo it.

In another incident, when I was showing a woman how to master her oral skills for her husband, on a reality TV show that was geared toward improving sex lives, I was just using my hands on a dildo to show her the movements and asked her to do the same. But she insisted on putting the dang dong that I was using for my demonstration in her mouth, despite me repeatedly asking her not to. Not only did it get seen by her family, her employer, her colleagues, members of her church congregation – this was an educational show after all – it remained available online until her kids grew up and saw it for themselves. Once something's out there in cyber-space, there's no turning back.

5. Be careful of the image you project – sometimes less is more.

In the movie *The Piano*, Harvey Keitel becomes quite taken by a tiny hole in Debra Winger's opaque, woolen stocking, because everything else is completely covered up. Apparently, the idea for the movie was conceived when a gentleman went to the Playboy Mansion and was more curious about the fully clothed secretary's body than all the gorgeous topless Playmates, wearing nothing more than the tiniest of G-strings.

The premise: since we're more curious about what we can't see than what is in plain sight, sometimes it's more powerful to leave something to the imagination, which has a way of filling in the blanks with our very own idealized fantasies. I can certainly vouch for it based on my personal experience. Several years ago, I was vacationing in a Hedonism resort, where I was the only one wearing a bikini in an otherwise nude resort. I wasn't doing it for the attention, but as it turned out I got a lot more than those who had put themselves out there. Truth be told, that did make me feel quite powerful, even though that wasn't my initial intent.

But whether or not you're trying to get someone's attention, beware that others will be noticing you as well. So make sure that you're mindful of unwanted attention and responses.

6. *Never compromise your reputation at work.*

You're dressed nice, putting your best foot forward, doused in adrenalin from that perfect blend of angst and ambition – all the elements of a perfect date, only we're talking about work. Then throw in some booze and the perfect ambiance – as in, a dinner meeting, or wining and dining clients – and you're looking at the perfect cocktail of ingredients to make the situation even more seductively captivating

Add to that mix the possibility of wooing and pursuing bosses and clients and the sexually powerful Diva is bound to come, since it's nearly impossible to hold her back in those moments, thanks to her primal instincts kicking in on top of everything else.

But if that sexual power play continues in the workplace, you could easily compromise your integrity, especially if you get promoted. Even though you may have legitimately earned your spot by merit, everyone will question how you got there, and possibly spite you for it.

Finally, if things don't turn out as hoped – worse, get out of hand – resulting in someone getting fired or transferred, a sexual harassment law suit could ensue, or vengeance could rear its ugly head. Either way, you're looking at a recipe for disaster.

So put your dab on, work your confidence, maybe flirt a little - within reason, without getting spotted by others – and you'll work your magic without anyone ever realizing what hit them. Once you climb the corporate ladder your boss will be kissing *your* ass, any way you choose.

7. *Never forget you're the ultimate focus.*

While it's important to focus on your goal if you're to strike bull's eye, the ultimate focus should still be *you,* and what you hope to gain using your sexual power. If you are just thinking victory at any cost, it's easy to forget / compromise yourself in the process.

It could cost you a lot more than you realize, especially if you started off with low self-esteem; because you can easily forget to prioritize yourself in that case. And where self-love is compromised, the whole sense of self gets fractured, which is the antithesis of sexual power.

At the end of the day, we want to ensure that we don't hurt or diminish ourselves while trying to gain power, since that would defy the whole purpose.

Conclusion

If you feel that your life is too small for your soul's desire, it's time to think big; to answer the call of your heart's longing for excitement, to satisfy your primal yearnings, and to feed your hunger for power.

And what better way to satisfy all that than by connecting with yourself, finding healing and meaning, and then capturing your power and releasing it into the world, to expand your life?

We owe it to ourselves to live an ever-growing joyous life of authenticity. If we walk away from that and all that our bra-burning grandmothers tried to do to buy our freedom, it would be a waste of our power and the equalizing force it can create, as far as countless opportunities go.

Carl Jung spoke of *individuation*: the lifelong project of becoming more nearly the whole person we were meant to be – what the gods intended, not the parents, or the tribe, or, especially the easily intimidated or inflated ego.

It's in our blueprint to grow, and enjoy the safe and playful negotiations which allow us to share with one another, in ways that we were meant to.

Other primates have no confusion around any of it, since they don't talk themselves out of their natural instincts, because of what they've been led to believe; so their system works.

Ironically, as a "sophisticated species" we bind ourselves by our own rules – even those which don't serve any purpose – and we continue to accept deprivation and endangerment, just because someone told us that it's acceptable.

The proverbial hand on stove would remove itself as soon as it sensed the burn, warning it of danger. But many women in abusive situations keep putting their hand on that hot stove, to see if it's cooled down, or if it will stop hurting, when they can see otherwise – all because of some archaic notion which told them they have no power; they have to make it work.

If we're to look at examples in the animal kingdom, we could learn a thing or two from felines, to help us handle disempowering situations: once a cat experiences a hot stove, it'll always avoid it at all costs, even when it's completely cooled down – not suggesting we go to the other extreme, but we should at least listen to what our instincts are telling us. It'll help us rise up, feeling empowered.

And we need to do this for our own sakes, without being swayed by either take on that proverbial hot stove. Blaming others also victimizes us and depletes our power.

Camille Paglia, author of *Sexual Personae: Art and Decadence from Nefertiti to Emily Dickinson* (36), refuses to take that stance. In fact, her outspoken rebellion against a common feminist line – "anything negative about a woman is strictly the result of stupid men and narrow-minded misogyny" – nearly cost her the publication of her book. Seven publishers and five agents rejected it before it saw the light of day, for that very reason. Paglia says:

> *"I almost resist using that particular 'F' word. ... Feminism has absolutely collapsed. There were real leaders when it began, but then it started to silence any voice of dissent. Like mine. I wouldn't subscribe to anyone's party line, and they didn't like that. It soon disintegrated into folly and insularity."*

Point being, instead of assigning blame to another group, thereby handing over our power, we should truly liberate each-other, just as feminism initially intended, to bring equality and solidarity to women.

Toward that end, we should embrace our sexual power – among other things – and take charge of elevating womankind, supporting each other to reach true equality, just as many other groups have done, through solidarity, fighting a battle that's worth fighting.

Sadly, too many women condemn each other instead of supporting one-another. In a recent article titled "Generation Sex: Irish women – Madonna's or whores?"(37) Norma Costello discusses how Irish women are facing an oppressor greater than the Catholic Church, when it comes to their sexuality – i.e., other women. She spoke to various young Irish women, some of whom expressed that they just want to experience pleasure without being called 'sluts' or 'skanks', or having their sexuality dictated to them. They feel confused since they're somewhere between the image of the Virgin Mother or the town bike. Costello says:

> *"The simple truth is that Irish women are damned if they do and damned if they don't. The media projects us as sexual predators, flaunting designer handbags and having threesomes while, in reality, we often navigate a difficult path between 'frigid prude' and 'easy slapper'.*

> *... A friend of mine complained recently that female sexual pleasure has always been hijacked, whether it's by men, the Church or the media. There is usually an umbrella group waiting in the wings to tell us the 'right way' to have sex as women. There is also massive objectification to contend with and whether or not our sexuality has always been part of the patriarchal male narrative.*

> *... Lucy Shah, a woman from Dublin, carried out research on Irish women who identified as bisexual. Lucy feels bisexual women face a huge level of judgment and prejudice in Ireland for not fitting into a socially acceptable sexuality. 'Bisexual females had the most negative self-perception,' she says. 'In my opinion, it's because of set ideas on female sexuality. If a guy hears you're bisexual, he'll proposition you for a threesome. Often lesbians think we're bowing down to the patriarchy and a*

lot of people think we're just non-committal and need to 'pick a side'.'

We're sexual beings, we're all either having sex, have had sex or are thinking about having sex. It's a bizarre world when we won't talk about it."

It is my hope that you're not only able to talk about your sexuality, but also be able to enjoy the force of your sexual power – without judgement. Then and only then will you be able to conquer all which stands in your way of becoming the Sexual Goddess that you were meant to be!

What are you waiting for? The stars won't align to begin your journey – they'll only align once you've begun. So start now!

DANCE LIKE NOBODY
IS WATCHING

LOVE LIKE YOU HAVE
NEVER BEEN HURT

SING LIKE THERE IS
NOBODY LISTENING

WORK LIKE YOU DON'T
NEED THE MONEY

LIVE LIKE IT IS HEAVEN
ON EARTH

About the Author

Rebecca Rosenblat, host of the highly rated TV show – ***Sex @ 11 with Rebecca*** – is a certified psychotherapist, relationship & sexuality therapist, sex addiction therapist, life coach, and educator, critically acclaimed as a TV and radio show host, author, advice columnist, and motivational speaker, responsible for changing many lives.

Through her various shows, monthly advice columns, and dating, relationship, sexuality, and self-esteem books and seminars, she has reached a captive audience of millions.

As such, Rebecca has become the face of practical advice with the media and constantly keynotes at various important conferences and events worldwide.

To learn more about Rebecca, visit www.DrDate.com, or Google her to access her thousands of international contributions. To view some of her show interviews, go to: www.RogersTV.com/SexAt11.

For true success, be sure to follow Rebecca's mantra: "It's your life, make it exceptional!"

Appendix:

25 Crucial Guy Facts Women Need To Know:

1. Guys don't mind messing up a friendship if it could lead to great sex; don't buy it if he tells you otherwise – if he was interested, he would've already tried to mess around with you by now.

2. Should you ask a guy out? Again, if he was truly interested, *he* would've already asked *you* out.

3. Why don't guys call when they say they will? Guys hate confrontation (think of what happens when you want to "talk") and will say whatever it takes to maintain the status quo when ending a conversation/date. Why get into it when you don't have to? Doubly so with someone you don't intend to see again!

4. Should you call him? If a guy hasn't extended the courtesy of phoning you, why would you want to chase that down? ... No, he didn't lose your number!

5. Sex is one of the greatest joys of a relationship – if your guy is keeping you from enjoying it, dump him, sell the damn bling he gave you, and use the money to buy vibrators for yourself and your equally under-privileged girlfriends.

6. Him slipping his penis into someone else doesn't *just* happen – it's well executed in the first degree – so no get-out-of-someone-else's-vagina free cards!

7. After a breakup, still having feelings for him doesn't in any way translate into still having sex with him – no matter *what* he says!

8. If the world just revolves around him, with every rotation you'll get more and more screwed – and not in a good way. Find someone who spends as much time thinking/worrying about you as you do him.

9. Bad boys are generally bad for you – don't expect one to suddenly turn into Mr. Right. But as far as Mr. Right-Now goes, look no further.

10. Whatever he says, it doesn't count if he just says it after/during/while-hoping-for sex, or when he's high.

11. Cutting him off isn't about making him miss you – it's about you discovering you're fine without him!

12. If he asks you to lose 20 pounds, lose him instead; that's losing approximately 200 pounds in a jiffy – will make for an interesting before/after shot, with you looking more confident than ever!

13. An excuse he makes is a polite rejection. An excuse you make for him is stupidity and perpetual self-torture.

14. If you've been dating for five or more years sans any form of commitment, chances are it'll never happen. If you want it, don't wait for it – get it from someone else.

15. Groveling like a pathetic, desperate fool never made any guy change his mind about a woman.

16. Doesn't matter *why* he left, the point is *he left*. Quit beating yourself up already by pushing for a reason – do you really want to know why he doesn't feel like seeing you ever again?

17. If you really love someone you want to make them happy, not sad. Take a hint from your gut feeling.

18. *Nothing* can keep a guy away from someone he truly digs – that includes busyness and fear of intimacy.

19. How can you feel worthy of love if someone is going out of their way to make you feel unworthy?

20. Life is tough enough; you don't need someone who makes it tougher – unless of course you're a masochist, in which case you might as well buy a doggie collar so your friends can stop worrying.

21. Think of yourself as the rule, not the exception – it will change your perception to reality.

22. "Better than nothing" is never a good enough reason to stay – there's *always* something better!

23. If he can't be bothered to tell you what's going on, according to him nothing special *is* going on ... between the two of you that is!

24. If the guy you dig would rather shop and cook with you than try to get you naked, he's *not* a keeper – he's just not that into you. Find someone who is!

25. If he's not into you, don't take it personally; and move onto someone who digs you!

Bibliography

1.   Hakim, Catherine, Honey Money: The Power of Erotic Capital, Allen Lane Publishing, 2011

2.   Wolf, Naomi, The Beauty Myth, Harper Perennial, Reprint Edition, 2002

3.   Meston, Cindy, Buss, David, Why Women Have Sex: Women Reveal the Truth About Their Sex Lives, from Adventure to Revenge (and Everything in Between), St. Martin's Griffin, 2010

4.   da Silva, Gabriela The Pleasure Is All Ours, Vintage Espanol, 2008

5.   Symons, Donald, The Evolution of Human Sexuality, Oxford University Press, 1991

6.   Haselton, Martie, Journal of Research in Personality, 2003

7.   Jong, Erica, Sugar In My Bowl: 28 Women On Their Best Sex Ever, Ecco, 2012

8.   James, E. L., Fifty Shades of Grey, Random House, 2013

9.   Oggas, Ogi, Gaddam, Sai, A Billion Wicked Thoughts, Plume, 2012

10. Kagel, Tamara Shayne, The Feminist's Dilemma: Why We Can't Stop Caring About How We Look, Huff Post Women, 2014

11. Veda, Mira, Intelligence Is SEXY... You Sexy Feminists, Huff Post Women, 2014

12.   Plank, Elizabeth, Beyoncé Doesn't Have to Choose Between Her Sexuality and Feminism, Mic news, 2014

13.   Ensler, Eve, The Vagina Monologues, Villard, 2007

14.   Jocelyn, Partying with Your Inner Bitch, www.mamagenas.com 2014

15.   Thomashauer, Regena, Mama Gena's School of Womanly Arts: Using the Power of Pleasure to Have Your Way with the World, Simon & Schuster, 2003

16.   Fisher, Helen, Why We Love: The Nature and Chemistry of Romantic Love by Helen Fisher, Holt Paperbacks; Reprint edition, 2004

17.   Berger, Daniel, What Do Women Want? Adventures in the Science of Female Desire, Ecco, 1St Edition, 2013

18.   Black, Dorothy, What do women want (in bed)?, www.women24.com

19.   Zacharias Ravi, Can Man Live Without God, Thomas Nelson, 2004

20.   Heimel, Cynthia, Advanced Sex Tips for Girls, Touchstone, 1983

21.   Brushwood Rose, Chloe, Camilleri, Anna, Brazen Femme: Queering Femininity, Arsenal Pulp Press, 2003

22.   Bedford, Terri-Jean, Dominatrix on Trial: Bedford vs. Canada, iUniverse, 2011

23. Symonds, Sarah, Having an Affair? A Handbook for the Other Woman, Red Brick Press, 2007

24. Muscio, Inga, Cunt: A Declaration of Independence, Seal Press, Expanded and Updated Second Edition, 2002

25. Katehakis, Alexandra, Erotic Intelligence: Igniting Hot, Healthy Sex While in Recovery from Sex Addiction, HCI, 1 edition, 2010

26. Gladwell, Malcolm, Blink: The Power of Thinking Without Thinking, Back Bay Book, 2007

27. Pfaus, Jim, Rats Can Have Fetishes Too, Behavioral Neurobiology, Department of Psychology, Concordia University

28. Fisher, Helen, Why Him Why Her: Finding Real Love By Understanding Your Personality Type, Henry Holt and Co., 2009

29. Argov, Sherry, Why Men Love Bitches, Adams Media, 6th edition, 2002

30. Coontz, Stephanie, Marriage, A History: From Obedience to Intimacy, or How Love Conquered Marriage, Penguin Books, Reprint edition, 2006

31. Zacks, Richard, History Laid Bare: Love, Sex, and Perversity from the Ancient Etruscans to Warren G. Harding, Perennial, 1995

32. Klein, Marty, Sexual Intelligence: What we Really Want from Sex - and How to Get It, Harper One, 2012

33. Rinaldis, Sophia, 9 Body-Shaming Behaviors We All Need To Stop, Mind Body Green, 2014

34. Katie, Byron, Loving What Is: Four Questions that can Change Your Life, Three Rivers Press, Reprint edition, 2003

35. Zimmerman, Jonathan, Sexual assault in the hook-up era, Newsworks, 2014

36. Paglia, Camille, Sexual Personae: Art and Decadence from Nefertiti to Emily Dickinson, Vintage Books, 1991

37. Costello, Norma, Generation Sex: Irish women - Madonnas or whores?, Independent, 2014

Manor House
905-648-2193